MW01227001

Purpose Driven Coaching

A model for Educators, Leaders, & Workforce Development Professionals

Quintrel Lenore

DEDICATION

For the second time in a row, writing a book has been more cathartic for me than I could imagine. My hope was to download as much practical coaching knowledge as possible while providing a big picture perspective to help youth, professionals, and organizations. Through the process of writing "Purpose Driven Coaching" I realized how gentle, loving, and graceful God has been in my life. To think that a little kid from Portsmouth, Virginia who barely graduated from high school and college could write a book like this blows my mind. I thank God that I get an opportunity to share these thoughts with the world. I thank God for providing me with a family that loves me and allows me to sharpen my coaching skills day after day. Thank you Lorayah, Isaiah, and Olivia for being patient with me. Thank you, mom and dad, for loving me, teaching me, and coaching me.

TABLE OF CONTENTS

Pur·pose

the reason for which something is done or created or for which something exists.

Driv·en

operated, moved, or controlled by a specified person or source of power.

Coach·ing

a partnership between coach and client where a coach helps the client to achieve their personal best and to produce the results they want in their personal and professional lives

OK, BUT LET'S TALK ABOUT SPORTS FIRST

I was in an organization-wide meeting during the time of my writing this book, and one of my coworkers was nudged to give a "hot take." For those that don't know what a hot take is, it is a piece of commentary, typically produced quickly in response to a recent event, whose primary purpose is to attract attention." The person's hot take was that "sports is overrated." I don't disagree with them as I realize we live in a very big world. There are many cultural artifacts, hobbies, passions, and events to engage in. Only some things will be appreciated by everyone. When this person commented that "sports were overrated," it was a very lighthearted moment as many of us rolled our eyes and bantered in agreement and disagreement. This person didn't shatter my world by what they said because I have other things that are much more important to me than sports—namely writing, recording music, working out, and watching other things on television that are not sports. However, sports are pivotal to me in that the opportunities I've come to have as an adult were afforded through my participation in sports as an adolescent.

My parents put me in baseball and basketball growing up. I learned about teamwork, focus, resiliency, and consistency through my experiences playing sports. God gave me the genetic pedigree to become a 6'5, 260 lb Division 1 football player. In my business, Lenore Coaching LLC, I partner with organizations where I serve youth through career readiness and workforce development programming. Many of the youth are what I'd consider "at-risk," where if they don't find an avenue in the workforce, they will likely have a future that is very grim and dark. Looking back at my adolescent years, though I came from a solid family structure with great parents, if it weren't for sports, my life could have taken a troubling turn. Sports is not my everything, but it is something to me.

Why am I talking so much about sports? You are probably thinking to yourself, "I thought this was a book about coaching." Sports are one of the best microcosms for life. It is literally an arena filled with so many teachable moments. As coaches, we need stories, examples, context, case studies, and arenas to help us be better coaches. I promise you that this is not a book about sports. I promise you that this is not a book about me. Purpose Driven Work was my first book, and when I finished writing it, it turned out to be an accidental memoir. Purpose Driven Coaching is story-driven, but it's not about my story. It's about all of us who are positioned to serve people. The lens from which I wrote this book is for those of you who serve as educators, leaders, and workforce development professionals. For all of these types of professionals, coaching plays a critical role. If you are not in a coaching role or have a job title that says "coach" at the end of it, no worries, you're still a coach in some shape or fashion.

Sports have shaped my identity as a person and have also led me on a pathway towards becoming a coach. For me, sports was a vehicle that got me to a dream destination. If you're reading this book, you are positioned to help provide a vehicle for someone who may desperately need it. Our workforce, our businesses, and our institutions need coaches. The places we work in have people that need your help. In order for our organizations to flourish, the people in them need to flourish. Coaches are the catalysts that make flourishing a possibility. Because God decided to make us in His image, we are people of purpose. We ask "why" questions all day long. We move because we're motivated by a deep "why." Our "why" determines if we'll decide whether or not we want to flourish. That "why" is our purpose. Coaches are instrumental in helping other people to align their purpose with the work they do. As coaches, we should also align our purpose with the work we do. I hope this book helps you to help others better themselves. I'm such a big-picture thinker, so I hope this book provides a zoomed-out perspective of how important your work is, but I also hope it is practical enough to improve your performance as a coach.

CHAPTER 1

WHAT'S THE PURPOSE OF COACHING?

A LESSON FROM THE SPORTS WORLD

In 2012, LeBron James secured his first NBA championship playing for the Miami Heat. This championship was layered with storylines that would be important for LeBron, his team, the NBA, and possibly basketball overall. For LeBron, this marked his first-ever NBA championship. He has served as the face of the NBA and arguably the sport of basketball for most of his 20-plus-year career. This is the same kid who was raised by a single mother in an under-resourced community in Akron, Ohio, who has also surpassed Michael Jordan as the face of the NBA. The same kid from Akron is now the all-time points leader, surpassing Kareem Abdul-Jabbar on February 7, 2023, with 38,387 points. Through his acrobatic dunks, no-look passes, or just by the combination of his size, speed, and sheer power, LeBron has become more than a basketball star but a person whose story inspires people from all walks of life.

Unlike the 2006 NBA champions, in which Miami won their first title, the 2012 one was different. Because of the greatness that is LeBron James, the 2012 championship was expected. For LeBron and many of his fans, the 2012 championship was more of a sigh of relief. To be able to associate winning with such an electrifying talent can now bring a temporary armistice to the pressure-filled battle for basketball glory. LeBron and his teammates were expected to win that year just like they were expected to win the year before. The year prior, the Miami Heat went up against the Dallas Mavericks, who were led by a less talented but well-led cast of NBA veterans. The 7-foot Dirk Nowitzki was nearly an unstoppable force of nature, with a midrange fadeaway jump shot that has propelled him to number 6 on the all-time list of points leaders. In 2012, though, apart from Dirk, Dallas didn't have top brand name athletes that held comparison to the likes of LeBron James or his teammates Dwayne Wade and Chris Bosh.

So what was the deciding factor or alchemy of factors that allowed LeBron James to hoist the Larry O'Brien Trophy for the first time in his career? For the first time in his career, LeBron was submerged into a competitive environment with accountability that only allowed for there to be one goal in mind—a championship. Success can be measured in a variety of ways in professional sports beyond simply winning a championship at the end of the season. Success for professional athletes can hinge on personal and organizational expectations, including ticket sales, attendance, brand deals, television contracts, media attention, and much more. The disappointment in 2011 for the Miami Heat and the lack of previous NBA finals success for LeBron James presented a hinge moment at this point in his career. I'm sure he enjoyed and continues to enjoy the fruit of his success and fame beyond that of winning championships, but one can argue that in 2012, no other goal mattered more for him than the NBA championship.

Another factor for Lebron's early championship success was coaching. Pat Riley, the President of Miami Heat basketball operations, and Erik Spoelstra, the Head Coach for the team, are arguably the most important people in LeBron James' championship success. These two men together created an intense environment for LeBron and his teammates, with a focus solely on winning a championship. Pat Riley is a 9-time NBA champion as both a player, coach, and as an executive. Erik Spoelstra was mentored by Pat Riley while serving as an assistant coach for the Miami Heat for roughly ten years until he was promoted to Head Coach. Under Spoelstra's coaching tenure, LeBron went to 4 straight NBA finals while winning 2 of those championships.

Sports, like many arenas of life, including business, education, or politics, have an end goal. These goals can look radically different depending on the industry, but at large, there is a goal in mind. For a Fortune 500 corporation, one goal might be to increase the profits of its shareholders. Another goal for that same company is to reduce the company's carbon footprint by

10% to help improve the environment's sustainability. In education, a school district might have the goal of increasing graduation rates year over year. A predominantly white institution (PWI) might have a goal of retaining more black Indigenous people of color (BIPOC) students on its campuses. In politics, a seasoned legislator might have the goal of increasing affordable housing within their district. For LeBron James and the 2012 Miami Heat, it wasn't good enough to reach the NBA Finals, they had to win it!

No matter what industry or arena, a good coach will help someone to manufacture an atmosphere conducive to success. Sports is an easy way for us to see the importance of coaching because sports serve as a microcosm of life. In life, most professions are not secured by tenure, but rather, individuals have to compete in some shape or fashion to prove their worth to their organizations. A salesperson competes with company quotas, benchmarks set by their boss, or comparative metrics set by other internal salespeople in the company. If the salesperson develops a track record of underperforming in any of the areas listed, they risk being let go by the organization. Salespeople sharpen their skills through feedback from their managers, previous meetings with prospective clients, training seminars, colleagues, and possibly a sales coach. Like salespeople, athletes work to improve their performance within their respective modalities, including gyms, practice fields, weight rooms, and courts, which are microcosms of what they might see in corporate America.

A sports coach serves her athletes by setting the atmosphere for practice with the focus on helping her athletes increase their intensity within the competition. To do so, she will turn the music loud in the weight room, so much so that the sound reverberates off of the concrete walls as her athlete intensifies their efforts while 808s bang in the background to their favorite song. Similar to the sports coach, the 10th-grade English teacher sets an environment of focus by taking his class on a brief walk around the school prior to a midterm exam. Because his class had a below-average cumulative performance on the previous exam, he wanted to try something new in order to decrease anxiety and increase mindfulness to increase class performance in the midterm exam hopefully. Though both of these professionals aren't exclusively coaches by trade, they used a critical coaching technique by manufacturing an environment to produce successful results for their clients.

CREATING AN ENVIRONMENT FOR SUCCESS

In March 2020, my family watched in awe and confusion, like much of the world did, as a public health crisis progressively unraveled before our eyes. As COVID-19 hit news cycles, my naive brain couldn't understand the brevity of what was really happening. From my privileged perspective, the idea of a global pandemic had no weight on my life, and I had no conceivable understanding of how this would impact me personally. I saw death tolls rise and polarizing information spread seemingly just as quickly and ferociously as the virus itself. Admittedly, for me, the pandemic was less about staying safe or sending prayers to friends and families who lost loved ones. Selfishly, the pandemic was more about an opportunity not to have to physically go to work. I was relieved to know that I physically didn't have to make the 20-minute commute to work in addition to the 1/2 mile walk from my parking spot to my office to sit at my desk to do 1 hour's worth of work spread across 9 hours. I could now work remotely and not have to iron the same five outfits in the morning that I wear every week to work. I could now see the love of my life all day long and have romantic conversations while my five and six-year-old kids played ever so quietly in the background. I could work from home, which meant that I would have more time to scale my private coaching business and weave in and out of my day job and my actual dream job with ease. No one told me that after one month, my fairytale work-from-home scenario, romantically engulfing marriage, #hustleculture Gary V side hustle extravaganza, and superhero dad mode fantasy would be just that, a fantasy.

As public schools in our area adjusted to virtual learning, my wife and I went from pleasantry to pressure. My wife became our resident professor as she juggled her own day job along with being the primary teacher for our children's virtual school. They say you appreciate your parents when you have kids of your own. Well, the same can be said about our educators. I am curious to know how they do it. I have so much appreciation and gratitude for the teachers, school counselors, administrators, and staff who help educate our children. I watched painstakingly as my wife tried her hardest to teach "new math" to our kids. If you think $2 + 2 = 4$, you're wrong. The "new math" will tell you that $2 + 2$ will first need to be divided by 0.5 and then multiplied twenty-two times minus 4 Harlem shakes in order to get 5. That's right, according to the "new math," $2 + 2$ does not equal 4.

In all seriousness, trying to teach your own kids while they wiggle in their chairs, roll their eyes, and get attitudes while tears pour out of their eye sockets was a joke. Oftentimes, when my son or daughter would get emotionally overwhelmed, I would be the one to have to change the environment. I would have to give my wife a break and allow her to take a step back away from the kids and from teaching. In those moments, I might throw a YouTube breathing exercise on to help my kids calm down. I also take my kids outside to go for a short walk so they can get some fresh air and get their minds off of their studies. This time would allow for my children's frustration to subside and allow for their minds to welcome back a little bit of reasoning. By changing the environment, I wasn't just giving my wife a break; I was coaching my kids so that they could do "new math ."I was coaching them by helping them to develop the neural pathways needed to do hard things. I was coaching them on resiliency, mindfulness, and patience, which are the real skills needed in order to be successful academically.

As someone who graduated high school with a 2.3 GPA at an early age, I adopted the idea that intelligence is something people are naturally gifted with while some aren't. It was when I got to college on an athletic scholarship that I realized success in academics is less about natural intelligence and more about learning how to learn. In the classroom, I began to compete with my peers the same way I competed against my teammates on the field. I learned about various techniques to retain information in the classroom as I engaged in my studies. The pandemic afforded my wife and I the opportunity to transfer those same skills we learned in college to help coach our kids in their academics. We created an environment and a rhythm that was conducive to learning so that they could succeed.

I don't know what arena you compete in. Whether you compete in corporate America, education, government, politics, nonprofit, or another industry, know that coaching is a skill set that you can utilize. That's right! Your job title doesn't have to have the word "coach" in it in order for you actually to be a great coach. The work that you do will require you to influence other people in some shape or fashion. Michael Jordan once said, "Talent wins games, but teamwork and intelligence win championships." Jordan didn't win his first NBA championship until 1991, which was after he'd been in the league for seven years. This means that he failed seven times prior to winning a championship. This also means that more than his natural talent and skill was needed for him to win a championship. He needed a team, and he needed a coach to help create an atmosphere conducive for success to take place. I want to say that, yes, Jordan is right in that talent isn't enough to win championships and that you do need teamwork and intelligence to win. However, coaches help the players realize and adopt the steps necessary for teamwork and intelligence to win championships. Some of the best athletes, executives, teachers, managers, and workforce professionals understand the importance of teamwork and intelligence. However, not all of them take the practical steps to influence the changes necessary to help their teams adopt the measures needed to win their respective championships.

THE FREEWILL FACTOR

In 2003, a rapper by the name of Curtis Jackson, also known as 50 Cent, took the hip-hop industry by storm. His debut album "Get Rich or Die Tryin'" sold over 12 million copies worldwide. To put that into perspective, the most listened-to album in 2023 sold just over 600,000 copies worldwide. That artist is Taylor Swift. 50 Cent's most popular song, "In da Club," is a certified club banger which has allowed him to garner success by having fans all across the world, land an unprecedented 1 million dollar contract at the time, and procure countless awards, including an MTV Video Music Award for Best New Artist. 50 Cent released a book titled "Hustle Harder Hustle Smarter," where he chronicles his story including his humble beginnings growing up in Southside Jamaica Queens, New York. While Curtis was just a kid, his mother was killed by gun violence due to her activities as a hustler and drug dealer. The environment he grew up in and the people he grew up with played a huge role in his decision to eventually become a drug dealer himself. In his book, 50 Cent talks about being motivated to financially provide for himself and have nice shoes as an adolescent. He was also driven by the flexibility to make money on his own terms and time, which drug dealing afforded him. As you can see, 50 Cent's environment exposed him to a certain idea of success, which he chose to pursue. Since he also grew up in New York, which is the epicenter of hip-hop culture, 50 Cent talked about being exposed to artists like Nas, Biggie Smalls, Wu-Tang, Jay Z, and hip-hop patriarchs Run DMC. He was inspired to transition from full-time street hustler to full-time hip hop artist in the late 90s and early 2000s, so much so that he positioned himself to be mentored by hip hop legend Jam Master Jay.

Curtis Jackson credited Jam Master Jay for his success as an artist because JMJ helped him learn how to structure songs, craft hooks, and incorporate melodies into his music. With his polished rap abilities, hard work, along with his street persona, or, as 50 Cent would say, his "damaged" aura, these ingredients would propel him to stardom. 50 Cents' success in the industry hasn't been relegated to just his music career. He has garnered success as an entrepreneur by selling his equity stake in Vitamin Water to Coca-Cola for millions of dollars. He has produced and starred in multiple films, including the box office hit "Get Rich or Die Tryin'," which grossed over $46 million. He has also created and executively produced the hit television series called "Power," which propelled the main character Amari Hardwick into stardom. With all of Curtis Jackson's success, he acknowledges one of the biggest disappointments is the lack of success in some of his neighborhood friends and hip-hop group mates in G-Unit. If you've listened to any of 50 Cents' early music, you can hear him ad-libbing the infamous name of his hip hop collective "Gi, Gu, Gi, Git, G-Unit," followed by his sinister laugh. Apart from 50 Cent, the G-Unit roster was primarily made up of Tony Yayo, Lloyd Banks, Young Buck, and The

Game. In 50 Cent's book, he highlights his biggest disappointment stemming from the lack of success from Tony Yayo and Lloyd Banks. These are two individuals that 50 Cent actually grew up with in Jamaica, Queens, New York.

In his book, 50 Cent summarizes that Tony Tayo was a "street guy," while Lloyd Banks was someone who expected the world to come to him. He writes, *"I learned that when things are moving very fast, and you're constantly being put in new situations and environments, most people tend to lean back into their old habits, not develop new ones. After years of begging, cajoling, and threatening them to start doing things differently, I had to accept that Yayo and Banks were not capable of doing much more than what they were used to. You can lead a horse to water, but you can't make it drink. Those guys had been standing by the well for years and were still going to die of thirst."* Despite both of 50 Cent's neighborhood friends, now hip hop group mates, being in the music industry and having the talent to succeed, they still didn't measure up to the expectations set by 50 Cent.

As a coach, we can learn from all sorts of industries and stories about the power of influence. Coaches are positioned to help their clients, co-workers, or students to succeed. The goal is to help those individuals by manufacturing an environment to help them achieve their goals. There is both an art and a science that goes into creating those atmospheres and building a roadmap to success for a coach's client. There is a tremendous amount of effort, skill, and strategy that goes into helping others to achieve their goals. Despite all of those efforts, there is still an obvious wild card at hand. That wild card is the free will, or power of choice, of the person that you are coaching. At the end of the day, people will choose what they desire most. Tony Yayo and Lloyd Banks had the opportunity to tour the world, spend lots of money, and be surrounded by all sorts of famous people. Despite all of the extrinsic motivations, they both made a choice for their lives that wasn't in alignment with what their mentor, 50 Cent, had for them. As a well-intentioned coach, you will have to understand that despite your best efforts, the choice will still be that of your clients to adopt the pathway before them.

SO...WHAT IS COACHING?

Coaching isn't the only tool that you should have in your toolkit. Even if you're a coach, there is a strong possibility that most of your work may require you to use strategies beyond coaching to help clients with their problems. When we look at Figure 1.1, we can see a relationship between coaching, counseling, consulting, and mentoring. If you ask most educators, leaders, and workforce development professionals, they would say they'd use all of these mediums in some shape or fashion within their role. Many of us might find ourselves weaving in and out of one of these four domains through the course of a day, week, month, or year. The last thing I want you to walk away with from this book is a bias that coaching is the superior medium to effectively serve people. It is not. There are times when the people we serve will need us to tap into one of these domains more than the others. However, a common mistake that professionals make is lacking the awareness to overuse or underuse one of the mediums.

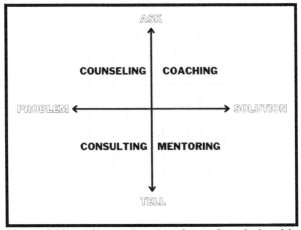

Figure 1.1 is an illustration that shows the relationship between coaching, counseling, consulting, and mentoring.

With coaching, the focus should be on asking the right questions in order to help clients find their own solutions. As coaches, you don't own the answer to the problem. The client does. We risk damaging the relationship with our clients by jumping in to solve their problems. Even more, we risk the possibility of our clients becoming codependent on people to solve problems for them, or we risk the possibility of the client developing the critical thinking skills necessary to solve their own problems. Your superpower as a coach is in your ability to ask the right questions at the right time. The conversation shouldn't be filled with a bunch of questions from us and responses from clients. There is plenty of opportunity for you to respond by sharing your experiences, contextualizing through storytelling, and giving best practices. Coaching is an art and a science, so there is a need for coaches to be aware of when to ask questions vs. giving input.

Counseling will similarly require practitioners to ask questions, but the heart of the relationship is to help solve a problem. Clients who struggle with anger management will see a counselor rather than a coach to help them cope with their problems. The nature of counseling will usually relate to an emotional or psychological challenge, but not always. The client and counselor relationship will usually focus on getting to the root cause of a behavior and then providing prescriptive solutions to address the problems associated with a diagnosis or trauma. The client and coach relationship is a collaborative partnership that is driven by enhancing performance for clients to accomplish a goal. Consulting is usually a contract-based relationship where a consultant tells the client a solution to a problem. Consultants and clients can be a person-to-person dynamic, but consultants will often partner with an organization. Consulting tends to be solution-oriented and tactical in nature, while coaching relies on trust-building and collaboration. A client or organization may have a variety of needs for which they would contract a consulting, including but not limited to:

- Market research
- Defining a problem
- Analyzing a performance challenge
- Solving a performance challenge
- Improve a process

Mentoring can be the most ambiguous of the four mediums as, most times, the individuals in a mentorship relationship rarely define the relationship. More often than not, people recall mentorship from people in their past rather than intentionally leverage people to be mentors. When individuals do use mentoring intentionally, the impact is undeniable. Often, a mentor is someone who speaks into another person's life by telling them unique strategies the person should take in order to be successful in a certain area. For example, a first-year college student may join a campus club and find a senior college student that they look up to. This person might not formally ask them to be a mentor, but they may ask to spend time with them on a regular basis. Throughout their time together, the first-year student might pick the senior's brain about the right classes to enroll in, which organizations to join, what to major in, and how to be successful in college. The mentor will usually give advice from their lived experience through the successes and failures they've experienced. They will usually give advice that is specific to the mentee because of the trust and intimacy that has been established. It is possible to have loose mentorship relationships that don't meet often or physically in person at all. Often, people will say they have mentors from afar that they admire but haven't actually met. I would argue those people are more of a role model or an inspiration rather than a mentor. Regardless of the title, all of these types of relationships and mediums are important to help people grow.

THE PURPOSE OF COACHING

The purpose of coaching isn't to make someone walk the path that leads to success. You can't make anyone do anything in life. If you are able to force your will on someone, then that relationship isn't coaching. It is something altogether more sinister. Rather, coaching is a cooperative relationship between 2 or more people. Coaching is a form of social contract where there is a clear benefit for the parties involved, yet there is an agreed-upon sacrifice that the individuals make in order to achieve a prescribed outcome. For the leader of an organization whose tendencies skew towards micro-management, adopting coaching skills will be a huge challenge for you. For the empathetic listener, who is ever so gentle and mindful with their clients, there are still some areas of growth for you as well. Both of these types of professionals can enhance their coaching toolkit to help manufacture success in their client's lives.

Let's not forget that being a coach is a huge benefit for you as well. This book will unpack the Purpose Driven Coaching Model that illustrates how important your role is. When I wrote Purpose Driven Work, the scripture from which the book was based was Genesis 1:28 (NLT), which says, ***"God blessed them and said to them, "Be fruitful and increase in number; fill the earth and subdue it. Rule over the fish in the sea and the birds in the sky and over every living creature that moves on the ground."*** As a human, but especially for us practitioners, this verse provides four areas where we can see the purpose of coaching. The four pillars of purpose include individual fruitfulness, population fruitfulness, territorial expansion, and territorial control.

You are walking in your purpose as a coach when you are producing fruit for yourself first, which is the 1st pillar. Dr. Eric Thomas is a mentor of mine from afar. I aspire to walk on stages and impact large audiences, similar to what he's doing. But I'm far from there. However, I know that I am individually fruitful because I can see evidence of my growth. To know where you are living out the 1st pillar of individual fruitfulness, you must ask yourself, "Am I doing the work that contributes to my personal growth?" As I mentioned, I'm a high school graduate who has a 2.3 GPA. I have since gone on to have a 15-year career in education, career coaching, and workforce development industries because I put in the work to better myself. I am confident in my skill set because of the years of sweat equity I put into practice, and I'm super pumped because I'm just getting started.

There is evidence that you're walking in your purpose when you can see population fruitfulness. Simply put, does the work you do contribute to the betterment of someone else? Most of us wouldn't be where we are if it weren't for some parent, teacher, mentor, counselor, or coach who invested in us. Those people who invested in you were exemplifying the 2nd pillar of purpose by helping you to get to where you are. We are standing on the shoulders of giants because someone poured into us, sharpened us, and helped grow our perspective. By the way, there isn't a timestamp to this. I can't tell you how many people have contributed to my growth by giving me a word of advice that lasted less than 10 seconds. So keep in mind you can contribute to the 2nd pillar of population fruitfulness in a variety of ways, and time isn't contingent on the impact you can have.

The 3rd pillar is called territorial expansion. In Genesis 1:28, God told the humans to *"fill the earth and subdue it."* Some folks might have mixed feelings or misconstrued thoughts when it comes to power. Power in and of itself is not an evil thing. Power isn't a good thing. It's just a thing. Unfortunately, our human history is riddled with horrible examples of humans leveraging power to do evil things. What isn't talked about too often is the importance of using power to do great things. Great things like the will of God on earth. A will that is focused on His glory alone being praised while we live harmoniously with each other, doing ridiculously creative things while we're here. Let's face it, Hitler was a bad guy. But imagine if his giftings in leadership, storytelling, and innovation were used in a way that was submitted to God's will and not his own perverted will? There is a purpose in spreading ideas, best practices, solutions, and innovations across the world.

Lastly, territorial control is the 4th pillar. Once we're able to champion ideas for the good of God's glory and for the benefit of humans living out our purpose, we just have to keep doing it. There is a constant fight to sustain goodness. Fortune 500 companies pay big money to retain market share. If a company has an innovative product that is doing well in the marketplace, you better believe their competition is charging their research & development department to come up with something similar in order to compete with them. If products and services are vulnerable to time, then you better believe that ideas do as well. As a coach, it is a part of your mission to partner with other mission-adjacent people to sustain territorial control in the arena that you serve in. Power can be a good thing to be utilized for territorial expansion and control for God's glory.

YOUR PURPOSE AWAITS

This book will be applicable to coaches and leaders across any industry. I've written this book so that the concepts are transferable no matter what your job function is or the people you serve. I am a Career Coach and Workforce Development Professional by trade, so it is my hope that this book can help folks effectively lead other people so that we can collectively enhance our workforce. When I was studying for my SHRM-CP exam a few years ago, a phrase stuck with me that I will never forget. The phrase is that "our organizations are vulnerable to change ."People come and go in our organizations. Legislature impacts the policies and processes we must enact in our organizations. Technology constantly innovates and forces us to adapt to how we do our work within our organizations. Sometimes, the mission stays the same, but no matter where we look, there will be forces that constantly pull us away from executing that mission. Despite our vulnerabilities to change, success is largely determined by our ability to coach our people through change. Coaching is not an exclusive tool, nor is it a tool that is more or less important than other skills. My hope is that this book provides a macro and micro perspective to utilize the Purpose Driven Coaching Model in our world of work. Let's be fruitful. Let's multiply. Let's subdue the earth through our purpose.

CHAPTER 2

THE PURPOSE DRIVEN COACHING MODEL

WALKING THE TIGHTROPE

When I wrote Purpose Driven Work, I had no clue what I was doing. I had never written a book before, but I knew I wanted to write about something that would help people in their careers. The heart of the book was focused on helping people get unstuck in their careers. I've seen too often how people let their dreams die because of barriers or obstacles that life brings. I also see people who achieve great success in their careers, but at some point, they realize they are still unfilled in their lives. There is an emptiness, a burden, or tension that many of us wrestle with when it comes to navigating our careers. At the time of writing this book, I am at a place in my career where I want my contribution to focus less on direct service to clients and more on serving the people who serve the clients.

I recently read a book by Stacy Spikes called "Black Founder: The Hidden Power of Being an Outsider." In his book Spikes chronicles his story from aspiring actor and musician, to hungry upstart music industry professional, to music industry executive, to movie industry executive, to eventually becoming the founder and CEO of his own publicly traded company. Through Spike's book, he tells his story from the lens of being an outsider. One of the ways that Spikes talks about being an outsider was at the early stage of his career. He worked at a media company that licensed racing videos for TV broadcasts and low-budget movie titles to various retail video rental stores. Though Spikes himself took acting classes and was an aspiring musician, he embraced being an outsider because he wasn't someone who had a successful career in Hollywood. At the time, he was an outsider to the entertainment industry because he was someone who was merely a gopher at a small media company. He was an outsider because his dreams didn't yet match the success of his dreams, which I'm sure many of us can relate to. The subtle gap between dreaming and actually having success is our commitment to the road towards success.

Early in Stacy Spikes's career, he committed himself to being a gopher at a no-name media company, although this opportunity was a far cry from the red carpet and flashing lights of Hollywood. As an outsider to the music and movie industry, he made himself available to his supervisor by learning the assortment of projects the company had to offer. Before the world of Canva or Adobe Photoshop, he was responsible for working with freelance artists and printing companies to materialize video covers for a multitude of low-budget films the company produced. Over time, Spikes built a rapport with the vendor who printed the video covers for the company he worked with, so much so that he'd spend a great deal of time hanging out and chatting with a colleague who worked there. During one of those times when he was hanging around, he overheard a conversation that a sales representative was having. He overheard that Berry Gordy had sold Motown to Universal Music and that the company was moving to LA and hiring. The sales rep turned to him and asked if he was interested in working for Motown and insisted that she could connect him with someone of influence at the company.

Eventually, Spikes would break into the music industry, working at MCA, formerly known as Motown, as a glorified gopher who helped to get album art approved. It is here where we can see an important component of purpose being illustrated. We must start. If you want to live out your purpose, then you have to get working. We must develop skills in order to walk in our purpose. I'm a guy that loves hip-hop music. If you've read my first book, Purpose Driven Work, then you'd know that I'm a part-time artist and full-time fan of hip hop. I'm at a stage in my life, though, where I am very selective about what I listen to since everything isn't always edifying to my soul. Because of that, one of my favorite artists is Lecrae. My wife and I went to his Church Clothes 4 tour when he came to Virginia, and we had a ball! We got VIP tickets, which allowed us to participate in a meet-and-greet session with Lecrae. It was there that he answered questions from the crowd about a wide variety of topics. One of the questions that someone asked him was,

"How do you balance being an artist, public figure, a husband, a family man, and your faith?" His response stuck with me and inspired how I will illustrate the Purpose Driven Coaching model in this book. His response was, *"I don't!"*

Life is so difficult no matter who you are and what you're going through. The consistent thing that all of us can come to expect about the human experience is that pain is inevitable. When Lecrae responded, he went on to talk about how he's learned that life is like walking a tightrope. If you can imagine being at a circus, you might see a trapeze artist or tightrope walker balancing on what seems like an invisible wire rope connected to two beams at a death-defying height. I'm afraid of heights, so I could never imagine standing on a three-story apartment balcony, let alone a tightrope hundreds of feet in the air. Going further, though, Lecrae talked about life being a healthy tension in which you walk on a metaphorical tightrope. When trapeze artists are walking on their tightrope, they look so composed, but if you look closer, there is consistent tension applied from their body mass and the rope they're walking on. Depending on the skill level of the tightrope walker, you will visibly see the rope continually making micro-shifts as the person negotiates their mass against the rope. This is the tension that Lecrae is talking about when juggling his life's affairs. As an artist, there is tension applied in one direction while his affairs as husband pull him in another. Through juggling and developing skills with leading his career, family, ministry, business, and more, he negotiates his life on the tightrope.

This illustration isn't exclusive to Lecrae. All of us have our own tightrope that we navigate in life. Chapter 1 used sports as a microcosm for life, so in building on that idea, there are various tightropes inside of our microcosms that we navigate. Inside your world of work at your day job or business, there are forces you must continually negotiate on your tightrope. It's possible that you feel the tension between being a leader of people vs. being a specialist at a project or skill set in your job. Maybe there is tension in the type of stakeholders you must interact with. Some stakeholders may require gentle nudging and clarification, while some stakeholders might require more intrusive support that takes a lot of investment to manage. As we go through this book, my hope is that we can unpack strategies and provide awareness that might lead to your fruitfulness as a coach.

THE PILLARS OF PURPOSE

This book is meant to help educators, leaders, and workforce development professionals to richly serve in their arenas of influence. Some of us will be positioned to provide direct client or customer support. Some of us will be positioned to steward the people and resources within an organization so that those organizations can continue to execute their mission. Some will be positioned in a variety of places between leadership and direct customer support to help organizations execute their mission. No matter what our roles are, the primary driver for success is purpose. From a macro-perspective, we can ask ourselves, "Is this company, department, business unit, or team doing what it is supposed to be doing?" From an interpersonal perspective, we can ask ourselves, "Am I doing what I am supposed to be doing?" Lastly, from an impact perspective, we can ask ourselves, "Are the people that I'm serving doing what they are supposed to be doing?" These questions are centered around purpose. Am I fulfilling my purpose?

As mentioned in Chapter 1, this book that you are reading, as well as my first book "Purpose Driven Work," were built on the scripture Genesis 1:28, which says, ***"God blessed them and said to them, "Be fruitful and increase in number; fill the earth and subdue it. Rule over the fish in the sea and the birds in the sky and over every living creature that moves on the ground."***

Based on this scripture, the 4 Pillars of Purpose include the following:

- **Individual fruitfulness** - The work I do is productive, helpful, and impactful for me
- **Population fruitfulness** - The work I do is productive, helpful, and impactful for others
- **Territorial expansion** - The work I do leads to the growth of organizations, institutions, and geographies.
- **Territorial control** - The work I do has consistent productivity and impact on organizations, institutions, and geographies.

Okay, let's address the obvious here. I'm using the Bible to unpack coaching principles and concepts that impact non-Christian arenas. The reality is that there are going to be many readers who are turned off by this, which is completely understandable. For those of you who might be in this predicament, I want you to understand that these concepts are not exclusive to Christian ministries, churches, or faith-based organizations. All of our organizations have the same problem, no matter the industry or size of the company. All of our organizations have to know what its purpose is. Many organizations can very well find themselves operating for a long time and have economic success without using the Christianese language and concepts that I'm discussing. However, when we zoom out and talk about eternal fruitfulness, longevity, and success, we can not escape the absolute truth. The reality is that God has a monopoly on truth, and anything outside of His purpose will ultimately fail. End of story.

If you work for a university or in the K-12 space these concepts might seem conflicting, especially for those of you that serve at non-faith-based organizations. Understand that these concepts might not be in alignment with the mission or culture of the organizations you work for, but these concepts are a framework that you can individually leverage on your mission while you serve the people at your organization. The Purpose Driven Coaching model is a matrixed framework that can be applied as individuals or collaboratively with fellow partners of the mission. I challenge you to see the big picture in our world of work. Our schools are meant to educate the future thought leaders and professionals that impact our workforce. In our workforce, we have a diverse representation of companies and industries whose purpose should hinge on making our planet and communities a harmonious place to live. We can walk outside, turn on the television, or look at our mini-feeds to see that this world is, in fact, not a harmonious place. Our communities are not equitable, safe, healthy, or sustainable for all of the folks that live in them. This means that our companies and institutions have to do a better job of fulfilling their purpose.

When we look at the big picture, we can easily see beyond the success of Amazon, Blackstone Inc., Harvard, McKinsey &

Company, and The Department of Defense. These organizations have impacted the lives of millions of people in a positive way; however, there is a greater purpose that is unfulfilled in our communities at large. This book isn't meant to solve macroeconomic or social problems that we face in our world. This book is meant to help equip people to do the work that aligns with solving macroeconomic and social problems in our world. The jury will forever be out on whether our collective purpose has been fulfilled as a human generation until we meet our maker. I digress, as that is a possible conversation for another book.

AN ILLUSTRATION OF PURPOSE

When looking at the illustration in Figure 2.1, you can see the foundation is built on God. He has a monopoly on truth and purpose. As people, we are created beings and are a reflection of God's creativity. Our purpose is wrapped up in glorifying God and worshiping Him. Many people have a church-centric perspective on worshiping God. When most people think about glorifying God and worshiping Him, they think about going to church on Sundays, singing songs, and vocally praising Him. These practices are parts of worship, but these practices are not an exhaustive list of what it means to worship God. Why am I talking about God so much, especially if I've talked about how this book is meant to help equip educators, leaders, and workforce development professionals? Well, that's because the work that we do to help coach our clients, generate profits for our businesses, and manage company resources is all a form of worship. Simply put, the foundation of the PDC model, as illustrated in Figure 2.1, is built on God.

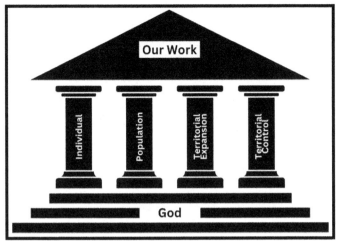

Figure 2.1 illustrates the Purpose Driven Coaching Model built on God as the foundation and our work being held up by the four pillars of purpose.

INDIVIDUAL FRUITFULNESS

For a high school teacher, individual fruitfulness will be crucial in order to adequately educate his students, but first, this teacher must have an impact on themselves. Educating and coaching people may be focused on helping people, but in order to first help others, there is some personal growth that must happen. This growth is related to believing in oneself, gaining confidence in one's abilities, learning specific subject matter, identifying what one might value in the work one does, and much more. These interpersonal skills are first fruitful for you. A high school teacher will have spent at least four years in college, along with likely having a graduate degree related to education. The courses and projects will allow him to learn about their interests, their values, and their strengths, which contribute to him being personally edified. Nick Cannon once said, "My vocation is my vacation. I love what I do." At the heart of this quote, you can easily see that the work he does is, first and foremost, something that he finds pleasurable for himself. This concept is for all of us.

If you've ever coached a student who didn't feel confident about a subject, it's easy to see how that experience is mutually rewarding for the coach and the student. The student doubts themselves. They don't believe they are smart enough to understand the material. They might make excuses as to why they don't have enough time to study the material. They might have even been resistant to receiving your help. But through your encouragement and persistence, they bought into your game plan to coach them in their studies. After a few times meeting with them or after a period of time working with them, they do it! They ace the test that you've been helping them to study for. Tell me this. Are you proud of that student? Are you proud of yourself? Hopefully, you said yes to both. This is evidence of the importance of individual fruitfulness.

When we think about the tightrope metaphor, a teacher will have to invest the time and effort to build confidence in themselves to get on the rope in the first place. When a tightrope walker first starts out in their craft, they can barely call themselves a trapeze artist or a tightrope walker. However, they have a vision in their head about becoming one. That vision motivates them to invest in themselves and practice. Through practice, failure, and perseverance, that person improves. They go from falling off the rope to maintaining a wobbly stance on the rope. Through practice, failure, and perseverance, they go from maintaining a wobbly stance on the rope to taking a few steps before falling off. Obviously, I have no clue how tightrope walkers become successful, but you get the point. Individual fruitfulness is the catalyst for any sustainable impact coaches will have on their clients. Individual fruitfulness is the precursor for a high school teacher leading his own class and serving his students. With individual fruitfulness, this means that the work I do is productive, helpful, and impactful for me.

POPULATION FRUITFULNESS

Individual fruitfulness is the catalyst that eventually fuels coaches to have an impact on people. Whenever we get a chance to help others, this is population fruitfulness. The Purpose Driven Coaching model isn't meant to be linear. Meaning that there are many times when a person can have population fruitfulness but lack in the area of individual fruitfulness. There will be instances where an organization has territorial control while a majority of the people in the organization aren't fruitful. When we think of population fruitfulness, this means that the work I do is productive, helpful, and impactful for others.

A Program Manager for a nonprofit workforce development organization may have a focus primarily on population fruitfulness. Her role is to help youth between the ages of 12 - 19 years to gain the career readiness skills necessary to achieve their goal in the workforce. In her role, she may lead programming that allows youth to intern with local businesses while simultaneously attending professional development workshops. The Program Manager will have a dynamic and comprehensive role where she may have to lead planning efforts, recruit staff members, manage payroll for youth workers, develop compliance policies, and much more. Providing direct coaching to youth probably isn't the primary responsibility or her responsibility at all. Her role may be to help create an atmosphere where youth can receive the coaching they need in order to help with their career development.

Population fruitfulness is the tightrope that the Program Manager will have to walk as she navigates a variety of forces on her rope. She will have forces associated with budget, staffing, staff skill set, availability of quality business partners and vendors, mindsets and attitudes of the youth, and much more. There are many forces this Program Manager is up against that make her walk on the tightrope that much more difficult. It is important to think of the tightrope as a metaphor where the stakes are rarely as high to the point where absolute failure is at risk. It is important to normalize adversity and failure as we walk our tightrope. We're going to fall off. When that happens, we can learn from it, adapt, get back on, and try again. For most of us, or for most of the time, there is a safety net underneath us that keeps us from impending doom. Certainly, there are work experiences where there are stakes that are very high. If you Google "tightrope walker," then you might find images of a person walking between 2 buildings with nothing but concrete thousands of feet below. Those are very high stakes! I don't want most of us to think that our work is so high stakes that failure seems insurmountable to recover from. Special thanks to members of our armed forces, where the stakes are quite high on the battlefield. If you coach in these arenas, then I think there should be an extreme level of intensity and attention to detail individuals should operate with. Walking that type of tightrope has little margin for error, and the stakes are high. However, most of us are not in those types of situations.

A Program Manager will flex population fruitfulness when she notices that 20% more participants go to college after completing her program in comparison to the previous year. Population fruitfulness can occur when her staff members report having increased confidence in their coaching skills with their assigned youth. Population fruitfulness can be evident when her business partners report decreased rates of tardiness or no-shows from their youth workers compared to previous years. Work that contributes to productivity, helpfulness, and impact on others is population fruitfulness.

TERRITORIAL EXPANSION & CONTROL

As professionals and entrepreneurs, we spend a great amount of time focusing on our individual aspirations and goals. From a professional standpoint, we must continually add skills to our toolkit just to stay employed, let alone have an impact on our organizations. For entrepreneurs, if you don't innovate and problem-solve, you won't have a sustainable business to maintain. Whether that means growing your business, stewarding your business's resources, or innovating on a product or service, business owners simply can't stay still. There is always a new legislature, new competition, new economic climates, new environmental limitations, or new technologies that force organizations to adapt. The work we do as professionals and entrepreneurs is never on an island. The work we do is in collaboration with someone else directly or indirectly. The high school teacher we discussed earlier might teach 8 History classes a year with over 100 students spread across those classes. He will lecture and test them on the History curriculum his school district provides, but he is doing fruitful work to impact his students beyond just teaching. He is mentoring, encouraging, nudging, clarifying, challenging, guiding, and coaching students so that they can one day be successful in the workforce. This same History teacher is one of 8 other History teachers at his school. The History Department of 8 teachers is one department of 30 other departments that comprise a high school with more than 60 teachers, administrators, and staff members. The work that the school does is collaborative as they serve their populations. Together, the professionals in that school have a territory they must continually work to control and expand.

We can define territorial expansion as the work we do contributing to the productivity and impact on organizations, institutions, and geographies. Similarly, we can define territorial control as the work we do having consistent productivity and impact on organizations, institutions, and geographies. It's funny because when I first started writing this book, I got all the way to chapter 6, and I started to get confused as to whether I had these two backgrounds. Initially, I had territorial expansion, then territorial control, and then I decided to flip the two, but then I finally put the two back in their original order. I wanted to be sure that the idea of the four pillars was in alignment with what the scripture says in Genesis 1:28. When we allow God to lead us, he usually takes us into a place we're not familiar with and therefore do not initially control. Many Old Testament stories showed a pattern of unqualified characters conquering new territories because of their dependence on God. The three ideas to think about when it comes to expanding and controlling territories are the importance of connectedness, influence, and sustainability. The purpose of territorial expansion and control is to align our purpose with the work that we do in collaboration with adjacent purpose-driven individuals.

CONNECTEDNESS IN YOUR TERRITORY

Connectedness speaks to the fact that our work isn't on an island. It's not just for us, but it's for other people. On top of that, the work we do isn't executed exclusively by us, but it's done in collaboration with others, which is also connected to various other value chains. A high school is part of a school district, which may have 10 to 50 other schools. One school may serve 2,000 students, but a school district will collectively serve 50,000 students. That school district may also be affiliated with

100 other organizations and businesses with a similar mission of educating and developing the leaders of tomorrow. Those 100 other organizations are connected by providing workforce development programming, social services, economic relief, or technology support to the students and key stakeholders associated with the school district. The teachers in that school district are not the exclusive contributors that expand and control that territory. That territory has tightrope walkers composed of Engineers, Lawyers, Administrators, Police Officers, Nonprofit Program Managers, and Career Coaches. The people in this territory may have other territories they are a part of, but in this territory, they are connected in their mission of educating and developing the leaders of tomorrow. Subdue and multiply!

INFLUENCE IN YOUR TERRITORY

Influence plays a crucial part in territorial expansion and control because people never stay the same. People are constantly absorbing ideas, thoughts, behaviors, cultural artifacts, and more. People are constantly being influenced in one way or another. Every day, we are either drifting away or closer to our purpose. Every day, we are either getting better or worse. As educators, leaders, and workforce development professionals, we must equip ourselves so that we can properly equip others. We are the influence for better or worse for the people we serve. If you've seen one of the Progressive commercials where Dr. Rick coaches a group of new homebuyers, you can see the power of influence on display. In the commercials, Dr. Rick helps the new homebuyers who seem like Millennials who have all of a sudden started acting like their Generation X or Baby Boomer parents. Some of the new homebuyers are guilty of not knowing what "sliding in someone DMs" are, unnecessarily cleaning outside trash cans, conducting awkward small talk to strangers, or asking too many questions about the options on a salad bar to the restaurant associate. My favorite is the guy on the elevator who does excessive small talk to random strangers because that is something my dad actually does. There is no such thing as a stranger to him. Although this commercial is really well produced and scripted, it shows a glaring truth to the audience. The power of influence. All of those new homebuyers, probably at some point in their adolescence, were annoyed by the idiosyncrasies of their parent's behaviors, but as grown adults, they inevitably became just like their parents. As coaches, we have to be mindful of the influences our clients have. We may have to help work to unravel the negative influences that keep our clients stuck. We may also have to proactively do individually fruitful work within ourselves to strategically influence our clients in a positive way. Subdue and multiply!

SUSTAINABILITY IN YOUR TERRITORY

Sustainability is the third principle that affects territorial expansion and control. A Program Manager at a Workforce Development organization may face pressure from key stakeholders to adapt her programming in a way that decreases the quality of the service provided. That pressure may come from budgetary constraints, cultural views from stakeholders, a lack of support from her leaders, and more. Sustaining a successful business model that supports Purpose Driven Coaching is less about maintaining the status quo. Sustaining the PDC model at an organization is more about strategically stewarding the resources and people to effectively keep your mission competitive with outside forces. Remember that good tightrope walkers appear as though they aren't struggling. However, they are constantly applying their body weight to the rope as gravity, wind, rope texture, and various other factors force the tightrope walk to negotiate their balance. Sustaining the territory that you and your collaborators serve in will consist of a multitude of factors that you all will have to negotiate. Subdue and multiply!

APPLICATION OF THE PDC MODEL

As I mentioned earlier, the Purpose Driven Coaching model isn't going to be for everyone. There are folks who will be turned off because of their own mindsets and convictions. We all are on our own journey and have the ability to freely choose the ideas and tools we want to adopt. However, I believe strongly that the PDC model is applicable to people from all walks of life. Whether you're a professional, an entrepreneur, a parent, a thought leader, or whoever, this model can help you to align your purpose to the work you do. This model will allow you to collaborate with people through a different lens. It will allow you to see the pain points in your organization from a different perspective. This model will help you to measure success economically and eternally.

The purpose of the work we do is inescapably built on God. No other foundation is sustainable. This means that no matter what type of work we do, it must be aligned with His will or it will inevitably fail. Dr. Tony Evans wrote a book called "Kingdom Men Rising," where he tells a story about the importance of a solid foundation. He and his wife noticed a crack in the wall in their bedroom. Like most wives do, she nudged her husband, Pastor Evans, to get a professional to check it out. Pastor Evans then proceeds to contract a painter to come to his home to paint over the crack to match the color of the rest of the wall. A few days passed, and Pastor Evans noticed the crack had re-emerged, to his surprise. He reaches back out to his painter to get the crack painted over again. Problem solved, right? Of course not. After a few more days, Pastor Evans was alarmed when he saw the crack emerge again, but this time, the crack was much larger and pronounced. Frustrated with the painter, he calls him to immediately come to his house to fix the botched job he performed multiple times at this point. The painter was surprised by Pastor Evans' passionate and frustrated curiosity as to why the paint job was botched. The painter responded to Pastor Evans that the problem wasn't the fact that the paint job was botched but that he had a bigger problem. The painter told him the real problem is that you have a problem with your foundation. No matter how many times I come out to paint over this crack, there will always be a bigger problem under the surface until you can fix the problem with your foundation.

Many of us and many of our organizations have a problem with our foundation. Many of us mean very well in our intentions to equip ourselves with the skills, methodologies, knowledge, and resources to do effective work. The effectiveness will indeed be impactful. However, without a foundation built on God, the effectiveness of the work we do will be limited. I don't know about you, but I get extremely excited when I get a chance to make a tangible change. When I facilitate a workshop for underserved youth in the inner city of Richmond, Virginia, I feel like I'm making a difference. I can teach these youth important lessons until I'm blue in the face. However, if the foundation I have isn't rooted in God, then my efforts will inevitably be voided. Some of us are looking at the cracks in our careers, business strategies, and organizations. Some of us see the inefficiencies, redundancies, gaps, and neglect, and want to focus all of our energy on those areas. The things we see aren't the root cause of the problem at hand. The foundation for our organizations and communities is jacked up. We must make sure we're addressing the right problem. The real problem and not the cracks that stem from the problem. The Purpose Driven Coaching model is a tool that will help educators, leaders, and workforce development professionals to align the work they do with true purpose. Subdue and multiply!

CHAPTER 3

PERFORMANCE IN THE WORKFORCE

PEOPLE MAKE ORGANIZATIONS VULNERABLE

Leif Babin and Jocko Willink are former United States Navy SEAL officers who wrote a book called "Extreme Ownership" where they discuss the leadership skills they've leveraged while serving in the armed forces. Their experience in dangerous combat zones fighting to protect the freedoms we get to enjoy has allowed them to parlay those experiences outside the military into corporate America. Officer Babin and Officer Willink talk about how their leadership consulting company, Echelon Front LLC, provided consultation to a financial services company whose CEO insisted that his company was in dire need of their "Extreme Ownership" coaching model. In the book, they write that upon visits with the CEO and various executive leaders, it became apparent that the company was in need of change because they were economically in the red. The idea of "Extreme Ownership" can be summarized as the organization's leader taking on all accountability for the personnel and the projects those people do within the organization. This concept was developed through Officer Babin's and Officer Willink's time fighting in Iraq and Afghanistan at the heart of the war on terrorism. These men and their teams fought in territories where the enemy was out to kill them and their teammates. The men experienced some of the harshest realities of life and death in all of the human experience. Babin and Willink discussed that while serving in a time of war, one decision they make as leaders can potentially lead to the loss of a human's life. When the stakes are that high, there is no other option except to take full responsibility as a leader. It is a requirement in order to be a leader. This concept of full responsibility is called "Extreme Ownership."

When Officer Babin and Officer Willink were meeting with the executives at the financial services company they were consulting with, most of the executives found it hard to adopt the idea of

"Extreme Ownership." These executives found it hard to be fully responsible for the success or failure because there were too many variables, such as their staff's skill level, nuances to communication plans, integration of technology systems, and uncertainty surrounding customer engagement. In the minds of those executives, there were simply too many factors to consider in order for them to be fully responsible for everything under their control. As Babin and Willink progressed through their leadership coaching program with the executives, all of them began to adopt the "Extreme Ownership" model with the exception of one person. The Chief Technology Officer (CTO) of the financial services company was vocally antagonistic to the concepts that Babin and Willink unpacked. As the men met with the CTO, his direct reports, and his colleagues, it became clear that most of the problems the company faced were because of the disruption that the CTO was actually causing.

Officer Babin and Officer Willink reported the progress to the CEO of how their leadership coaching was going with the executives. They pointed out that the company would not be successful unless the CTO completely bought into the changes that they were implementing. The rest of the executives were on board, but the CEO felt reluctant to confront the CTO about their resistance. Essentially, Officer Babin and Officer Willink gave the CEO a warning that if he doesn't make a decision about the CTO, then his hard work growing his company will eventually fail. Sensing the severity of the situation at hand, the CEO eventually fired the CTO because of their unwillingness to take on complete accountability for leading his team.

"Extreme Ownership" is a great model and skillset to adopt. However, I actually want to emphasize something much more subtle than a coaching model that greatly impacts the success of organizations. Through Officer Babin's and Officer Willink's leadership coaching, it is apparent that organizations are vulnerable to change because of the people who work in them. I'll say that again, organizations are vulnerable to change because of the people who work in them. Success and failure literally hinge on people. The presence of the CTO of that financial firm played a significant role in why the company was in the red. We live in an era where Fortune 500 companies compete for market share by the smallest of margins. Companies will invest millions of dollars in technological innovations, external consulting to improve processes or contract a staffing firm to recruit the needed talent, all so that the company can remain competitive in the market. I want to focus on the performance of people and unpack how imperative it is to provide the coaching needed to help people make an impact in the Workforce.

SKILLS PAY THE BILLS

In my company, Lenore Coaching LLC, we have a career readiness program for youth called "Momentum." This program has six core content areas that I lead participants through. This program has been implemented with middle school students, high school students, college-aged students, as well as adult learners who have been in the Workforce for up to 30 years. The concepts that I unpack are comprehensive and relevant to every person, no matter what age group, so that they can be successful in the Workforce. One of the content areas focuses on work skills. In almost every session, I passionately tell participants, "Skills pay the bills!" The National Association of Colleges & Employers (NACE) has eight competencies that speak to the importance of skills in the Workforce. These competencies are:

- Career & Self-Development
- Communication
- Critical Thinking
- Equity & Inclusion
- Leadership
- Professionalism
- Teamwork
- Technology

We often use competencies and skills synonymously, but I want to make sure I distinguish between the two so we can understand how to effectively coach individuals to perform in the Workforce. **A skill is the ability to use one's knowledge effectively and readily in performance.** For example, a career changer had two different career coaches this past year. The career changer said that both of her coaches listened to the challenges she had in her career. However, she said the 2nd coach helped her get better clarity on her career goals because they helped her process the right pain points that she needed to discuss. We can see that both career coaches used the skill set of active listening, asking questions, and problem-solving. However, the second career coach had a higher level of active listening, asking questions, and problem-solving compared to the first coach. People may have the same variety of skills at their disposal, but each individual person has a varying level of ability to flex those skills.

A competency combines skills, behaviors, knowledge, and abilities that enable an employee to effectively perform their job. When we think about the NACE competencies listed above, think of those as domains in which a variety of skills will be needed to perform that domain. For example, teamwork competency will require a Program Manager at a Workforce Development organization to flex the following skills, behaviors, knowledge, and abilities:

- Coordination skills for recurring team meetings with stakeholders
- Active listening skills to assess the needs of stakeholders
- Behave empathetically in areas of conflict between stakeholders
- Have knowledge of motivational interviewing to resolve conflict between stakeholders
- Have the ability in a busy schedule to invest in resolving conflict

You can see from the five bullets above that competencies are dynamic, comprehensive, and allow for performance to be evaluated in a nuanced way. One of the challenging things that organizational leaders are faced with is having to train their employees in these competency areas. It is possible for people to be trained on certain work-related skills, but it is much more difficult to train a person when it comes to behaviors. For example, when we think of cultivating empathetic behaviors, people will have varying levels of intrinsic relatability to this behavior. As leaders and coaches, we must assess the skills associated with behaving empathetically. Empathetic behavior may consist of skills such as vocal encouragement, displaying receptive body language, actively listening, and much more. However, we must understand that there might not be an ideal benchmark for coaching behaviors because of biases. In some cultures or people groups, empathetic behavior may look totally different than others. We have to be careful not to perpetuate a systemic bias where the benchmarks are standardized by a supreme culture, race, or ethnic identity. In order to maintain an inclusive culture while still developing the performance of our organization's talented people, coaches must emphasize skills. Skills pay the bills!

COACHING SKILLS

When I graduated college with my bachelor's degree in Kinesiology, I entered the Workforce as a Sports Performance Coach. I spent the first four years of my career helping student-athletes in a college setting. I worked with some of the best athletes in the country, serving in various Sports Performance roles, including Bridgewater College, Mississippi State University, James Madison University, and Shenandoah University. Prior to beginning my career in college Sports Performance, I was a former student-athlete at James Madison University. As a student-athlete, I loved training. I loved the technical aspect of weightlifting. One of my favorite exercises to do as an athlete was the Clean. There are a few progressions of the Clean, including Power Clean, Hang Clean, Jump Shrugs, and more. When I was an athlete, I enjoyed doing the lift, but I didn't have very good technique compared to my fellow teammates. I struggled to get underneath the bar to finish the lift. In other words, it was easy for me to generate the power using my core, hips, and legs to get the weight moving upward. However, when it came time for me to catch the bar, I struggled to transition my weight underneath the bar to finish the exercise. My skill level at this time of my life had a threshold. My coaches spent time with me on my technique. They gave me verbal feedback. They even demonstrated the exercise multiple times to help me improve my technique. However, I never saw an improvement in my skill level with this exercise while I was in college.

When I decided that I would become a Sports Performance Coach, I had to attain three core certifications to help me become more knowledgeable and qualified in the industry. I became certified through the Collegiate Strength and Conditioning Coaches Association (CSCCA), National Strength and Conditioning Association (NSCA), and

USA Weightlifting (USAW). The USAW certification was the most practical and influential certification when it came to improving my skill level with Olympic lifts. Over the course of 3 days, I learned how to effectively demonstrate and teach a Clean, Snatch, and Jerk. For the Clean in particular, the coaching I received from the instructor was so intensive, individualized, and intrusive that it allowed me to enhance my skill in executing the exercise. I tell this story because although this example is talking about physical coaching for skill development, the lesson still applies wherever.

If organizations need their talent to have a growing proficiency in soft skills or technical skills, then they will have to coach them. In the information technology industry, common skill gaps include coding, cloud computing, cybersecurity, mobile application development, data analytics, machine learning, and network virtualization. Not having enough skilled technical professionals in those areas leaves organizations vulnerable. Companies need people to do the work necessary to execute their mission. If organizations don't have qualified talent or sustainable talent with cybersecurity skills, then the information a company fights to protect will be vulnerable to hackers. The average cost for a data breach in United States companies is 9.48 million dollars. The cost to recruit an employee who has the skills to prevent those data breaches can range from $4,000 to $20,000. This seems like a lot of money, but in comparison to what's at risk for the company, it is well worth it to recruit skilled talent.

The challenge that many organizations face isn't getting qualified talent that has the necessary technical skills in the door. Rather, the challenge organizations face is keeping them. The most common reason why it is hard to keep qualified talent isn't that they want to jump ship to another company for a bigger paycheck, but rather they leave because of issues surrounding company culture. This company culture is largely determined by how well the individuals in the company work with and treat one another. Certainly, leaders set the tone by exemplifying the cultural practices they want their employees to mimic. At the heart of those core cultural practices are soft skills. Soft skills are character traits and interpersonal skills that characterize a person's relationships with other people. Here are some examples of poor usage of soft skills that cause conflict and frustration in organizations:

- Direct supervisors excessively micro-managing talented workers with proven leadership skills
- Team members reacting emotionally over differing opinions about a project
- Team members bickering with other team members because of unresolved conflict
- Individuals acting passive-aggressively when a customer vocalizes displeasure with their service
- Individuals miss a project deadline because they didn't prioritize deliverables on multiple projects
- A team fails to meet company OKRs because a manager didn't train their team properly on a new process

So, how do you coach talented individuals in your organization to develop the skills needed to perform? Individuals have different learning styles, preferences, and abilities when it comes to learning a new skill. Coaches and leaders should have a process but also a mindset that embraces the variability of how people learn new skills. When coaches are teaching new skills, they should first explain the concept. Explaining the concept will give workers an overview of the new concept. Explaining the skill will allow the worker to hear and synthesize the information you're telling them. The second step is to demonstrate the concept by physically demonstrating the skill. This often allows individuals to contextualize the idea. The demonstration takes the concept and puts it into practice, which gives the worker a more in-depth understanding of how to execute the skill. The third step is to let them actually practice doing the new skill. I would argue that this is the most important step. The difference between education and developing skills is practical application. We've heard the phrase "seeing is believing," I would argue that "doing is succeeding." The last step to coaching a new skill is to provide feedback on how to perform the skill. This is probably the most common visual that folks would have when they think of a coach. Coaches should provide verbal feedback to correct or enhance how workers perform the skill. For coaches who are trying to help workers perform in the Workforce, it is important to individualize the best strategy for providing feedback to individuals. Coaches help individuals develop skills by explaining, demonstrating, letting them practice, and then providing feedback.

EDUCATING VS. DEVELOPING SKILLS

Professionally, I've spent most of my career working in Higher Education or in an education-related field. I've experienced firsthand the power that education has on an individual's life and perhaps the life of their family members. On average, the quality of life looks much different for a person with a college degree in comparison to a person without one. The opportunity for career advancement and career variety increases for individuals with a college degree in comparison to individuals without one. For folks between the ages of 22 - 27 with a college degree, the average annual salary is $52,000 compared to $30,000 for those folks without a college degree. There is no question how valuable it is for a person to receive an education as it pertains to their success in the Workforce. From the organization's standpoint, many companies spend a great amount of time and money to recruit people with college degrees. It was difficult for me to determine the percentage of effort that organizations spend to recruit recent college graduates vs. experienced professionals. However, I did find that 90% of employers prefer to hire graduates based on real work experience rather than their educational background. I want you to make sure you catch what I just said, though. Yes, organizations spend a great amount of time and money recruiting college graduates, but why is that?

Changes in the Workforce have rarely been immediate but rather progressive over time. I've worked in Higher Education for nearly ten years, where most of my work didn't require me to be

45

onsite. However, it wasn't until a global pandemic that my organization's leaders found it fitting to usher in work-from-home policies. The point that I'm trying to make is that it often takes high stakes for organizations to make necessary changes. Should organizations have educated employees or skilled employees? Both. Should organizations stop focusing on hiring talent based on whether they have a degree? Not necessarily, but organizations do need to take a deeper look at hiring talent for the right skill set vs. just focusing on those with college degrees. Many colleges and universities are doing a great job of building real-world work experience into their curriculum. For many other degree programs, especially those in humanities and social sciences, there is limited real-world work experience that students get. This means that many students will leave college with an education that is rich in information but lacking heavily in skills relevant to the Workforce. As educators, leaders, and workforce development professionals, this presents a rich opportunity for us to fruitfully impact individuals, populations, and or territories.

GAINING MOMENTUM

At Lenore Coaching LLC, we've partnered with high schools, workforce development organizations, and local government agencies to deliver comprehensive career readiness and workforce development programming. One of our programs is called "Momentum," where we facilitate content to youth between the ages of 12 - 19 years old. Our program has served over 500 youth participants over the past four years through soft skills training, career exploration, goal setting, and much more. Our program is unique because we're intentionally not trying to do the mission by ourselves. There are countless coaching businesses, internal workforce initiatives in schools, and insulated departments in government agencies that are all doing great work, but they're doing it on an island. I've worked at multiple universities that have career advising departments and initiatives on their campus, but they operate in such a way that they seem to compete with one another. I've worked for a state government agency that helped veterans transition from the military to the Workforce, but the primary OKRs were to outperform other veteran service organizations. I've seen it time and time again where workforce development programming becomes a community of divided effort vs. one that is collaborative and fruitful. We've partnered with the Mayor's Youth Academy (MYA) in the City of Richmond, Virginia for the past 3 years serving roughly 400 youth participants. Most of the youth who participate in our program come from underrepresented and underserved communities with an average family income of $40,000 annually. Many of the participants live in subsidized housing where their families make $10,000 - $15,000 a year. Our partnership with the Mayor's Youth Academy combines career readiness with real-world work experience. The team at MYA coordinates efforts for youth to work with 1 of nearly 50 community partners that include transportation companies, government agencies, financial institutions, retailers, and more. At the heart of this partnership, the participants gain the education and skills needed to become successful in the Workforce.

WHAT ARE YOUR STRENGTHS?

This summer, my wife and two kids did a family activity to enjoy the great outdoors here in Richmond, Virginia. Richmond is strategically situated on the James River, where it is not uncommon to see folks fishing, canoeing, swimming, and whitewater rafting. Yes, Richmond is the only urban city in Virginia that has whitewater rafting through its downtown area. The part of the James River that I took my family to was called "Pony Pasture." At this part of the river, you can literally walk across it. There are huge rocks randomly situated near one another and many right on top of each other that make it possible for people to walk across. At the Pony Pasture juncture of the James River, the distance from one side of the river to the other is roughly a quarter mile wide. Most adults or individuals with enough physical dexterity can make it across the river. So when I took my family to Pony Pasture in my mind, I thought it would be cool for us to venture from rock to rock across the river. However, as we got about 25 yards into our adventure, I quickly realized that although my wife and I could make it across, it would be extremely risky for our eight and 9-year-old children to make it across. All of us were uniquely endowed with physical characteristics that made the adventure challenging. For me, I had the rangy extremities, coordination, and power to leap from rock to rock with ease. My wife didn't have the same athleticism as me, but she was also rangy with her long arms and legs that allowed her to timidly scale across the rocks. My son, though not as tall as my wife, had enough athleticism and ranginess to get across the rocks. However, my son is an infamously nervous child when it comes to new things. His fear inevitably crippled him when it came to scaling rocks that were far apart. My daughter has yet to fully grasp the concept of fear, which is scary. Though she wasn't afraid to scale across the slippery rocks, her limbs weren't as rangy. She lacked the balance and coordination the rest of us had to scale the rocks.

So why do I tell this story about my family jumping on large slippery rocks attempting to cross a river? A person's strength plays a huge role when it comes to accomplishing a mission. Each of us has unique strengths that influence if or how we accomplish our goals. As a coach, you should understand that you have a unique set of talents that set you apart from other coaches. Coaches can serve in the same fieldwork with the same population but have a very different way of making an impact. Coaches must also be mindful that the people they serve have their own strengths. When we are helping people, we must take into consideration how their strengths should inform their path and how they travel that path. In the case of my family crossing the river, I certainly had a vision for all of us to get across the rocks to the other side. However, everyone in my family had unique strengths that positioned them closer or further from the goal. If you are a leader of an organization, then you have to be strategic about the people you're leading on the mission. Are all of them positioned to succeed? How can you help position them to succeed? If they are not positioned to succeed, then in what way can coaching help them to succeed?

CLIFTON STRENGTHS

During World War 2, Don Clifton was a navigator and bombardier flying B-24s on 25 missions. His contributions to the United States armed forces landed him a Distinguished Flying Cross for his heroic efforts in serving his country. After having served in a war that contributed to the death of nearly 15 million military personnel and over 38 million civilians, Don Clifton decided that he had seen enough things that were wrong in the world and wanted to contribute some good to humankind. This vision led him on a path to studying human development at the University of Nebraska-Lincoln after he left the military. In his studies, he realized that the field of psychology focused on what was wrong with people rather than what might be right with people. Clifton and his colleagues founded the Nebraska Human Resources Research Foundation, which served as a community service to students and a laboratory for graduate students to practice strengths-based psychology. This new strength-based approach to research conducted countless studies, including one that showed how successful students had notably different character traits than less successful ones, which would be an idea he'd continue to build upon.

Nearly 30 years later, in 1988, Clifton helped start a company called Selection Research Inc. (SRI), which focused on customer research and personnel selection. This company would eventually merge with Gallup, which was known for poll-related instruments. During this time, Don Clifton developed hundreds of predictive instruments that could identify top performers for specific types of work that could be helpful for organizations. By 1999, Clifton launched the StrengthsFinder assessment, which focused on individuals identifying their natural strengths, which began with 18,763 people completing the assessment that year. As of 2023, more than 30 million people have taken Don Clifton's strength assessment.

The Clifton Strengths assessment is important for coaches because it allows us to focus on maximizing the talents that a person has rather than fixating on people's weaknesses. When we were kids and brought home a report card that had two A's, two B's, and one C, our parents would likely spend more time trying to figure out how to bring up that C grade. There is nothing wrong with trying to improve our weaknesses. However, based on Don Clifton's research, we'd see exponentially more improvement in performance when coaching emphasizes developing the areas we're more talented in versus the areas we're least talented in. In the book "Strengths Based Marriage" written by Jimmy Evans and Allan Kelsey, they highlighted a study conducted by a school in the 1950s related to reading retention. The head of the school wanted to tackle some challenges they had noticed with incoming first-year students who struggled to retain the information they were reading in their studies. So, they organized two groups based on the student's talent level for reading retention. They assessed that group one read an average of 90 words per minute while group two read an average of 350 words per minute. After putting the students through a six-week intensive reading program, they reassessed the student reading retention rate. The students in group one increased their average reading retention to 140 words per minute, while group two students' average reading retention increased to a whopping 2,900 words per minute.

As coaches, if we can harness the power of positive psychology through a simple tool such as strength-based coaching, we'd see fruitfulness in all four pillars of the Purpose Driven Coaching model. The growth and fruitfulness we see relate to us as coaches and to the clients we serve. As coaches, it is important to understand that many of us will operate in the same arenas and do the same type of work, but because of our strengths, we'll execute our methods differently. I heard a quote that said, "If there are two of us, then one of us is not needed." Our strengths make us different from one another and will ultimately be a huge difference maker for the impact we'll have within our worlds of work.

Executing	Influencing	Relationship Building	Strategic Thinking
Achiever	Activator	Adaptability	Analytical
Arranger	Command	Connectedness	Context
Belief	Communication	Developer	Futuristic
Consistency	Competition	Empathy	Ideation
Deliberative	Maximizer	Harmony	Input
Discipline	Self-Assurance	Includer	Intellection
Focus	Significance	Individualization	Learner
Responsibility	Woo	Positivity	Strategic
Restorative		Relator	

Figure 3.1 shows the 4 themes that each talent resides in. Copyright © 2000, 2019 Gallup, Inc. All rights reserved. There are 8 - 9 talents in each theme category for Clifton Strengths

When you look at Figure 3.1, there are 34 total strengths across 4 themes. It is important to understand that when we talk about Clifton's strengths, we're really talking about talent. Clifton defines talent as a naturally recurring pattern of thought, feeling, or behavior that can be productively applied. Earlier in the chapter, we discussed the importance of developing skills. Talents and skills are different, but they have a positive correlation with one another. A person may be talented in the relationship-building theme. They may naturally show empathy and positivity when coaching others. Through practice, feedback, and development in the utilization of their empathy talent, they can become more skilled at using it. Just because someone is naturally talented doesn't mean they are proficient at using the talent. We've heard the saying that "practice makes perfect," but my kids taught me that a better way to say it is "practice makes progress." This means the more we practice our talents, the likelihood increases for us becoming better or more skilled at the talent. The increased proficiency in how we use our talents is where Don Clifton says our talents actually become strengths.

Strengths-based coaching is a coaching method within the Purpose Driven Coaching model. Simply put, Strengths-based coaching is when coaches lean into their natural strengths and help others leverage their strengths to perform in the Workforce. If a coach is trying to help a post-high school graduate to establish a career, they might be able to provide career clarity through assessing their top 5 strengths. At the beginning of the coaching process, the coach might start by helping the young person see which aspects of their strengths most resonate with them. This is called "Naming it." From there, the coach would ask questions to see which strengths or aspects of each strength the person believes to be true about themselves. As coaches, no matter how impactful we think our tools and methods are, we must understand that the client is the one responsible for taking ownership of their strengths. There are going to be parts of their strengths they believe to be true and parts they won't. This part of the process is called "Claiming it." From there, the coach could ask questions or do some exercises to see how the young adult would want their strengths to be best used in the workplace. They could use past experiences from school, part-time jobs, extracurricular activities, or community involvement to get context for how they've used their strengths. The coach can use that context to contrast that to potential careers in order to see how they'd like to use their strengths in their future world of work. This process is called "Aiming it."

The example above was Strengths-based coaching in the context of career clarity. You can use strength-based coaching in a variety of coaching arenas, including Executive coaching, Confidence coaching, Relationship coaching, Academic coaching, Leadership coaching, and much more. The application of Strength-based coaching inside of the Purpose Driven Coaching model can be applied in any arena. As coaches, we can affirm ourselves by assessing how we are individually fruitful, impacting population fruitfulness, contributing to territorial expansion, and championing territorial control. Core questions we can ask ourselves when using Strength-based coaching methods within the Purpose Driven Coaching model include:

- Am I using my strengths in a way that is physically, mentally, emotionally, and spiritually healthy for me?
- Am I using my strengths in a way that helps others to be physically, mentally, emotionally, and spiritually healthy?
- Am I using my strengths in a way that helps people perform better in the workplace?
- Am I using my strengths in a way that contributes to the success and sustainability of the organizations I serve?

Stephen Shields was my Clifton Strengths coach when I was going through my certification process with Gallup. He said, "Individuals are sharp, and teams are balanced." If you are an educator, leader, or workforce development professional, it is tempting to see your strengths from a negative perspective. We should all have self-awareness and be receptive to growth as we look to improve our performance in the Workforce. However, all of us will have more talent in certain areas compared to others. You might have more strengths in the "Executing" theme and feel like you need more strengths in the "Relationship Building" theme. You may have more strengths in the "Strategic

Thinking" theme and feel like you need more strengths in the "Influencing" theme. When you work with teams or are coaching people to work with teams, it is important to emphasize the idea of collaboration with other people and the idea of leveraging other people's strengths. If you feel as though you're lacking in the "Executing" theme, well, how can you partner with team members who are more talented in that area? Strengths are meant to be leveraged in partnerships, teams, and communities. We are better together. Finally, it is important to understand the idea of coupling strengths with other strengths. In scenarios where you need to make strategic decisions but lack talents in the "Strategic Thinking" theme, you may couple talents in your "Influencing" and "Executing" themes in order to get strategic things done. Clifton Strengths is a great tool, but please understand that you are too dynamic of a person for one tool to dictate how you perform. You possess the ability to use this tool to your advantage in a way that is best fitting to you.

INTRUSIVE VS. DEVELOPMENTAL COACHING

The leader of a local Boys & Girls Club (BGC) oversees programming, staffing, and budget for the organization. This local BGC chapter is positioned in a metropolitan city with more than 225,000 residents. Of those residents, roughly 15,000 live in subsidized housing. This BGC is nestled closely to lower-income neighborhoods, which also consist of large portions of those residents who live in subsidized housing. The programming for the Boys & Girls Club is geared towards serving the needs of the middle school and high school students who live in that area. Common programming needs from those students include but are not limited to the following:

- Career readiness
- Entrepreneurship & Workforce Development
- Academic Enrichment
- Literacy
- Social & Emotional Skills
- Art & Creativity

The leader of the Boys & Girls Club supervises five full-time staff members and roughly 20 part-time staff members consisting of job functions such as Bus Drivers, Field Service Coordinators, Youth Development Professionals, Operations Support Specialists, and more. The Field Service Coordinators (FSC) and Youth Development Professionals (YDP) are the primary staff members who work directly with the school-aged youth that patronize the Boys & Girls Club facility. These staff members usually engage groups of 5 to 20 students through a variety of activities that align with the program initiatives listed above. For many of the Field Service Coordinators and Youth Development Professionals, this is the first time they've provided direct support to youth. Their roles are critical in the youth's overall experience at the Boys & Girls Club but are also critical for each youth's personal development. At times, FSCs and YDPs serve as mentors and coaches to the youth participants.

The leader of the Boys & Girls Club conducts semi-annual surveys with the youth participants to gauge how their experience is going at the center and to get feedback on the programming and interactions with staff members. The leader noticed some disturbing feedback on the survey pertaining to how the youth engaged with the staff members. The areas of concern included:

- A "Dissatisfied" ranking on a 5-point Likert scale pertaining to the level of support provided by staff members to the youth
- A "Not Comfortable" ranking on a 5-point Likert scale pertaining to the level of comfortability youth had with talking to staff members.
- There were multiple comments in the survey from youth related to not feeling comfortable talking to staff members.

The leader was alarmed because, historically, the Boys & Girls Club is known for having staff members who have done a great job creating a safe space for youth to engage with them. After doing interviews with students and staff members, the leader decided to provide professional development to enhance coaching and mentoring skills in her staff members in order to tackle the challenges from the survey. Because the leader had very little bandwidth for a comprehensive coaching program with her staff, she decided to use her own discretion for which staff members she would spend most of her time and attention.

Of the 20 staff members, she decided to have bi-weekly individual coaching sessions with 2 Field Service Coordinators and monthly small group coaching sessions with 6 Youth Development Professionals. The structure and content in the individual coaching sessions and small group coaching sessions were similar as the leader focused talking points on but not limited to:

- Building trust with youth
- Finding common interests with you
- Mindfulness & awareness with you
- Using Cliftonstrengths in your role

For the individual coaching sessions with the 2 FSCs, the leader assigned individualized homework to each of them. After six weeks, the leader decided that 1 of the FSCs had displayed substantial improvement in their performance and also received positive feedback about the FSC from a few of the youth. For the other FSC, the leader felt like they still needed to receive coaching. The leader felt their performance had not improved and actually showed signs of regression in their role. The leader put the underperforming Field Service Coordinator on a performance improvement plan, which included meeting with a more tenured staff member who worked at the center. The small group coaching cohort concluded after three months of monthly meetings, as all of the participants had shown significant improvement in their performance.

The leader utilized intrusive and developmental coaching methods to help improve the performance of her staff members. **Intrusive coaching is a method that coaches utilize when clients don't fully understand how to solve a problem by their own efforts**. In this scenario, the leader displayed varying levels of intrusiveness with her staff members. For the 2 Field Service Coordinators, both were initially receiving the same level of intrusive coaching. After 1 FSC responded to the coaching methods, the leader determined they didn't need intrusive coaching anymore. For the other FSC, the leader increased their intrusive coaching efforts because they didn't respond well to the coaching. The leader also used intrusive coaching with the small group, but you can argue that this was at a decreased level of intrusiveness. We can argue that having the Youth Development Professionals join a small group is intrusive because they wouldn't have made the effort to improve their performance without coaching being prescribed as an intervention.

Developmental coaching is a method that coaches utilize to help clients take gradual ownership of a specific problem. The goal of the individual coaching and small group coaching the leader employed was for all of the staff members to take ownership of their performance. The survey results showed that the staff members needed a coaching intervention; otherwise, their performance would have continued to remain the same. The leader showed developmental coaching with the Field Service Coordinators by giving them individualized homework that would nudge them to take gradual ownership of their performance. She also used Intrusive coaching by selecting two staff members to meet with individually since she could have easily met with all of her staff members in a small group setting. The individual meetings served as evidence that a more intrusive method was needed for the 2 FSCs. Intrusive and Developmental Coaching are not interdependent on each other. Coaches can use both methods at varying degrees and scenarios. Intrusiveness speaks to the "closeness" or how "hands-on" a coach gets with a client based on the coach's perception of their client's "ability" to make the necessary change to solve their problem. Developmental speaks to the "tactical strategies" a coach employs in relation to "how much weight" a client is willing to carry to solve their problem. Examples of intrusive coaching include:

- A career coach meets with a cohort of clients individually each week for six months to discuss career clarity.
- A school teacher meets with a small group of specific students each day after class for a week to tackle college application processes.
- A nonprofit organization executive meeting with her cabinet team as a small group prior to a board of visitors meeting

Examples of developmental coaching include:

- A career coach gives some cohort members a homework assignment to network with professionals in their field of desired interest and gives the other cohort members a homework assignment to brainstorm a list of professionals they could network with
- A school teacher provides a sequence of steps with deadlines for the students to take to complete their college applications.
- A nonprofit organization executive assigned specific tasks for her cabinet members to complete for their collective presentation and report to the board of visitors meeting.

Coaching is both an art and a science. Helping individuals to perform in the Workforce contributes to all four pillars of the Purpose Driven Coaching model. This chapter is meant to give coaches a comprehensive look at how they might serve in their arenas. You are wired and crafted in a unique way that no other person is, so when you take into consideration the concepts proposed in this chapter, be sure to do it in a way that is authentic to you. This doesn't mean that your authenticity should compromise your growth or the sweat equity necessary to grow. Please don't make that mistake. I've seen plenty of professionals refuse to take accountability and ownership of their growth. At the end of the day, they not only put their clients at a disadvantage but they undermine their potential for fruitfulness in all four pillars. Sometimes, we don't see the end results of the work we do as coaches. Sometimes, we don't see how our work contributes to the bigger picture. But have faith that enhancing your competencies, enhancing your skills, using your strengths, being intrusive, and being developmental will help others to perform in the Workforce, which contributes to an impact in the Kingdom!

CHAPTER 4

CAREER NAVIGATION

EVERY PROBLEM STARTS WITH AN IDEA

It is the early 2000s, and Martin Eberhard wants to buy a sports car. As a successful electrical engineer and the creator of the world's first eBook, Rocket eBook, Martin has earned the right to buy a sports car. Not to mention, by this time, he's coming out of a divorce, so Martin has most likely worked up a huge appetite for something new. Something fresh. Something fast. However, as an inventor and an engineer, Martin has his ears to the streets. The streets being all of the nuances of the global economy. To be specific, around this time, there was an energy crisis. The United States has just declared war on terrorism and has commissioned military assaults in Afghanistan and Iraq to secure the U.S. more oil….I mean, protect us from terrorists. Sips tea. Around this time, the price per barrel of crude oil is on the rise. News outlets are also covering stories about Ozone depletion and the rise of global temperatures. So Martin starts to think to himself, "Do I want to buy another gas-guzzling European sports car that is bad for the environment?" Martin's wheels are starting to spin. And yes, this pun is intended and brought to you by the sponsors who want to help make this book a New York Times bestseller.

Martin decides to have a conversation with his friend Marc Tarpenning, who is also an engineer and co-founder of the company that made the world's first eBook in partnership with Martin. Martin asks Marc about the idea of creating a sports car. Because Marc is an engineer and a friend, his response isn't like most friends who would say, "Dude, why don't you just buy a sports car?" Nope, his brain is different from most of ours, so he actually humors the idea of creating a sports car. But Martin doesn't want to create any kind of sports car. He wants to create a car that is good for the environment. He wants to create an electric sports car. Martin's fascination with electric vehicles brought him on a trip to the EV1 by General Motors. Martin realizes there is a huge gap in the market because the EV1 does not look like a sports car, but rather, it looks like one of those flying saucers from 1950s sci-fi movies. Not to be confused with the DeLorean vehicle created by DMC, which was featured in the Back to the Future films. No, the EV1 won't cut it. If you Google a picture of Martin Eberhard, he won't necessarily exude the ethos of "swag," but he's got enough sophistication in his pours to want more than a clunky-looking space car. So, what do engineers do in situations like this? They take ideas and build prototypes.

A prototype always starts with an idea. The motives behind an idea are endless. Some people build prototypes because they want to solve a problem. For Martin, he wanted to flex on his ex-wife. For you, the sky's the limit! Simply put, a prototype is the first of something. It is typically a preliminary model of something from which other forms are developed or copied. Martin had a unique problem that he was interested in solving. Up to this point in history, there wasn't an electric vehicle that was high-performance and open to the market for consumers to drive. General Motors discontinued and recalled all EV1 vehicles in 2000. For Martin and Marc, this was a wide-open market that was untapped with much potential.

As educators, leaders, and workforce development professionals, we have a huge opportunity to serve people through career navigation. For those of us who are in positions where we're trying to recruit and retain top talent, it might seem contradictory to coach someone to navigate their career. Helping someone to navigate their career, who you would hope stays with a company and provides value for a long time, might seem like you're shooting your own self in the foot. For those professionals or entrepreneurs who actually provide career coaching, helping people to navigate their careers might already be second nature. No matter what type of role you serve, it is important to see the value in helping people with career navigation. For those of you who are reluctant about providing career navigation coaching to your employees, understand that helping them clarify their future career goals will increase their performance, increase their engagement, and keep those workers at your organization longer.

In my book Purpose Driven Work, I've talked about how people get stuck in their dreams, callings, and careers for a variety of reasons. Some people don't have a "why." Some people don't have a greater purpose that propels them to perform in their world of work. Other people lack general clarity about the type of work they are called to do. For many other folks, they might get stuck because of physical and mental barriers that life throws at them. Similar to Martin Eberhard's motivation to build an electric sports car, we must also be moved to build prototypes with our careers. Whether we use these tools for ourselves or to help our clients, building career prototypes will always help us to get unstuck, gain clarity, or find our why. When it comes to you or your clients, we must first generate an idea before we build a prototype. For careers, what ideas do you have? Said another way, what problem are you trying to solve in your career? Many of us get stuck because we don't know what we want. For Martin, he wanted a sports car that looked good and was good for the environment. There wasn't anything available to him on the market, so his idea forced him to start to solve that problem. His idea forced him to build a prototype.

THE PROTOTYPE PROCESS

Martin and Marc were on a mission to create an electric sports car that looked good, was good for the environment, and drove fast. Their journey brought them to a company called AC Propulsion that was about to go out of business. Through Martin's research, he heard that AC Propulsion fabricated Go-Karts and small vehicles. Martin found out that the company used lead-acid batteries to power their small electric vehicles. With Martin's own money, he contracted AC Propulsion to create an idea that was in his head. He gave them the specifications for the design of the car. Underneath the hood, he used the lead acid battery technology that AC Propulsion currently had. Martin Eberhard and Marc Tarpenning gave birth to their prototype, Tesla. More specifically, TZero, the original prototype that the gentlemen created for their eventual company, Tesla.

When most of us think of Tesla, the first thing that comes to mind is Elon Musk. Elon Musk, in his own brilliance, can be credited as a technologist, investor, CEO, and founder of SpaceX. However, despite him being the most successful CEO of Tesla, he is not the founder of the company. Elon Musk isn't even the first CEO of the company but rather the 4th. I emphasize this not to throw shade on Elon Musk but to iterate that if the Prototype Process was used to create and grow a company like Tesla, then it can also be used to help people lead successful careers. The Prototype Process can be illustrated in Figure 4.1.

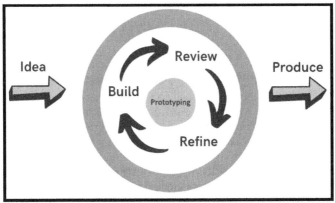

Figure 4.1 is an illustration of the Prototype Process created by Lenore Coaching LLC.

Step 1 is the "Idea' phase. As a coach, we and our clients will always have to start career navigation with an idea. That idea could be the desire to have a job with a certain salary. That idea can be to have a career in the Information Technology field. That idea can start with a general interest in a certain type of work. That idea could start with the desire to travel the world. That idea can start with the desire to have flexibility in one's work life and personal life. There could be one idea or a thousand ideas combined together that will initiate the Prototype Process for our careers or our client's careers. As coaches, it is our role to create an environment where those ideas can freely flourish. We can do that by asking the right questions, by nudging, by being intrusive, and by being developmental. In step 1 of the Prototype Process, there are no such things as a silly idea. The purpose of the Prototype Process is to strategically clarify and develop that idea into its intended fruitful outcome. What that outcome is to be determined.

Step 2 is the "Build" phase, which begins with what I call the "Cycle of Prototyping." In the Cycle of Prototyping, there are 3 phases, which include build, review, and refine. The Cycle of Prototyping can happen tens, hundreds, thousands, or millions of times. There isn't a specific amount of times that a person can go through the Cycle of Prototyping. Like an engineer, a coach or client will iterate on their career "idea" until they arrive at the product or solution they desire. In Martin's case, his TZero prototype would eventually lead to Tesla's first car model, the Roadster. In our careers, the product we're aiming for in the Prototype Process could be a dream job, launching a business, landing a contract, completing a work milestone, completing a company merger, and so much more. I want to emphasize that as coaches, we will have to clarify the career idea and the career goal. The build phase can start with an entry-level job that leads to future opportunities. The build phase can start with researching a list of dream jobs. The build phase can start with a Cliftonstrengths assessment or any career assessment. The build phase can be an internship, enrolling in a certification, enrolling in college, talking to a career coach, or anything that leads you in a forward direction toward your goal. The goal of the Prototype Process is to make forward progress and to get unstuck in our careers. There's a saying that I like, "Slow motion is better than no motion." The build phase is about putting things into motion no matter how fast or slow the iteration.

Step 3 is the "Review" phase. Simply put, whatever you've built, it's now time to take a look at it. At this juncture, we have to ask ourselves, "How can I improve what I have in order to get to where I want to go." Coaches will have to use good judgment on how to critique the clients they work with. We want to make sure progress is continual, but the reality is that some folks take constructive feedback very hard. When Martin and Marc built the TZero, they were proud of their prototype, but they knew they were far from launching a successful product or business. At this point, they didn't even have a legal business. Tesla wasn't legally incorporated at this point. The lead acid battery they used in the prototype was unsafe. If their car had been sold to the public, they would have risked the lives of many people as their car would've inevitably exploded. Once they built the TZero, they had to review other battery options. At the time, Dell computers were known for using lithium-ion batteries to power their computers. They took that idea and ran with it. They would test a combination of lithium-ion batteries to see how many it took and under what conditions it was safe to power an electric sports car. After much review, they would eventually get the internal parts of the electric vehicle up to snuff, including the battery, motor, and electronics. However, they had no clue how to fabricate the outside of the car in scale for the public. They'd have to partner with a company called Lotus, which is based out of the United Kingdom, to manufacture their Tesla cars. Keep in mind that all of this took money to do. Money they didn't have. In the review stage for our careers, it can seem like you're very far away from your actual goal. Sometimes, as coaches, we have to help our clients not focus on the end goal and focus on taking one step at a time. Build something, and then review what you've built. Keep it simple.

Step 4 is the "Refine" phase. In the refine phase, the goal is to make necessary changes based on what you've reviewed in the previous phase. Once Martin and Marc built the TZero, they realized fairly quickly that the lead acid batteries in the prototype needed to be replaced. They knew that the safety measures weren't going to comply with the industry standards to produce and sell vehicles. They knew they needed to find an option. Upon review, when they thought about lithium-ion batteries as a replacement for the lead acid option, they refined their prototype. Though they probably had hundreds of other specifications they reviewed and refined, they only focused on iterating one thing at a time. As coaches, help your clients refine one thing at a time. If I want to break into the Cybersecurity field, I have to start somewhere. I have to build from somewhere. The first thing I might build is my education or knowledge base in order to break into Cybersecurity. I may need to get a certification, take a course, watch a YouTube video, or get a degree. This is its own part of the Prototype Process that you will have to build, review, and refine. You might go through the education attainment part of the Prototype Process, but then you realize that you might also have to gain experience and skills. Maybe at some other point in the process, you realize that you have to expand your professional network to get exposure to career opportunities. I give these examples to show that the Prototype Process is meant to have multiple cycles for the same goal. Every cycle represents you getting better in some shape or fashion. Tesla has gone through millions or probably billions of Prototype Processes in order to produce their models, including the Roadster, Model S, Model X, Model 3, Model Y, and the Tesla Semi truck.

Step 5 is the "Produce" phase. This is the end goal you're shooting for. For Martin and Marc, they wanted to create an electric sports car. It is safe to say they accomplished their goal. However, other goals developed along the way. As these goals and visions come about, it is important to separate and prioritize them. Martin and Marc created a company called Tesla. To get funding to develop their car and incorporate a business around the car, they needed to partner with investors. Elon Musk was the earliest and biggest investor in Tesla. Martin was the original founder and the first CEO of the company. I don't know if he imagined being a CEO, but along the way of creating an actual prototype vehicle, a new goal of being a CEO materialized. Since the company now had a lot of new stakeholders, public expectations, multiple investors, and a board of directors, the expectations were shifted a plethora of times for Tesla as an organization. Martin would eventually be voted out as the CEO. Martin and Marc would maintain an undisclosed amount of shares in the company, but I'm sure it was disappointing for both gentlemen to be pushed out of a company that they created. We can take this lesson for our careers also. Your goals and needs change as you go through the Prototype Process. By prioritizing your goals, it can keep you focused on the things you want the most. There are very few things you can control in life, and the Prototype Process is a tool to help you manage expectations, navigate external obstacles, and make progress on the things you want in your career. Coaches will be instrumental in helping clients to achieve their goals using the Prototype

Process. Please keep in mind that as educators, leaders, and workforce development professionals, your primary role might not be that of a career coach. However, if you incorporate the Prototype Process into your role, you can strategically use career coaching to maximize your primary mission as an educator, leader, and workforce development professional. Subdue and multiply!

BE DANGEROUS

The single most impactful book that has transformed how I navigate my career and entrepreneurial journey is a book written by Jon Acuff called "Quitter: Closing the gap between your day job and your dream job." I read the book in 2021 in a season where my primary focus was scaling my business so that I could leave corporate America and work for myself. Up to that point, I had worked in Higher Education and Workforce Development for about ten years. In that season, I would work my 9 to 5 job as a Program Manager helping veterans to transition from the military, then come home and work until about 10 p.m. career coaching my own clients for Lenore Coaching LLC. I was excited that I was building something beyond what somebody's company could provide me. I saw a vision of autonomy and financial success as I was working with my own clients. Around July of 2021, I was working with the most clients I'd ever worked with at the time. But then I tore my Achilles tendon playing basketball. At first, this was the best thing that ever happened to me. This gave me a chance to build out the infrastructure for my business, including payment systems, websites, social media, business development plans, webinar content, sales funnels, and more. Since I literally couldn't move as my wife had me relegated to a certain downstairs portion of our house, I now had all the time on my hands to knock out this necessary grunt work. I was able to work with more clients and knock out all of these administrative pieces.

After a month or so passed, I began to get depressed. No matter how much work I put in, my company wasn't growing nearly as fast as I would have liked. Since I was sitting on my butt all day, I consumed an unhealthy amount of social media. The same YouTube videos from Gary V, Alex Hormozi, Dr. Eric Thomas, and Ruslan that motivated me to keep grinding on my dreams began to make me resent my dreams. I saw old classmates from high school and college seemingly explode with their personal brands and businesses. Inside, I was saying to myself, "Dang bro, you ain't nowhere near their level." In the words of Mark Manson, I began to contribute to my own "feedback loop from hell." So, I decided to stop taking clients. I decided to stop posting content on social media. I decided to stop reaching out to potential clients and business partners. In transparency, as I write this book, I still haven't fully recovered from the trauma that I put myself through in that season.

Jon Acuff's book began a journey of reassessing my personal goals. In the book, he talks about the importance of being patient with transitioning from your current job to your dream job. Acuff chronicles his journey as a professional, entrepreneur, writer, speaker, and published author. He talks about how his performance in his day job contributed to his job hopping and, at times, being let go. There was always something with the job or organization he worked for that left him unsatisfied. He started a blog that allowed him to flex one of his passions, writing. Even more so, blogging gave him an outlet and a vehicle to find his voice. This outlet allowed him to dream. Jon's talents as a writer, speaker, and thought leader eventually led him to land a speaking engagement at Dave Ramsey's headquarters. While there, Jon made an impression on Dave Ramsey and his team, so much so that he was offered a job. The job wasn't his dream job, where he envisioned being a full-time author, speaker, and creative. Jon would pass on the job offer and go back to his boring day job. He would continue to blog and share his thoughts with the world on a consistent basis. His blog continued to grow so much so that the public attention from it led to him being invited back to speak to the Dave Ramsey team. After doing a great job again, this time, he was approached with a different offer to work at Ramsey. He was invited to be a full-time author, speaker, and media personality. This was really his dream job!

Jon Acuff chronicles that the first ten years of his professional career working unfulfilling jobs taught him a valuable lesson. Because Jon had a stable day job that afforded his wife and children the consistent financial support they needed, it allowed him to "Be Dangerous" in his creative and entrepreneurial pursuits. Jon was picking up speaking gigs, consulting work, and creative projects over the course of 10 years while working his day job. His day job allowed him to be dangerous because he could dream big dreams when it came to his side hustles. If I ever get a chance to meet Jon, I would like to personally thank him. I'm at a stage in my career where I have a huge vision as a creative and an entrepreneur. I started Lenore Coaching LLC in December 2019, and every year since then, I've experienced incremental progress with the business. I'm not on Instagram or YouTube famous like so many of my peers. Starting back in July 2021, I have slowly relinquished the unnecessary pressure and expectations to be successful like the folks I see on social media. Because of my day job, the work I do outside of it allows me to be dangerous. I've implemented workforce development programs with youth who live in poverty. I provide career coaching to youth who live in some of the roughest neighborhoods in America. I've facilitated leadership training for senior-level administrators for a university. I've facilitated leadership training for human resources professionals for a publicly traded company. I graduated high school and college with a 2.3 GPA, and yet I have a book that is a part of the curriculum for workforce development programs. None of this would be possible if I didn't dream dangerous dreams, as suggested by Jon Acuff. None of this would've been possible if I also didn't relinquish the crippling expectations from people on social media.

As coaches, the idea of being dangerous is important for us and for our clients. Your journey as a coach is unique from anyone else's. The Purpose Driven Coaching model provides four pillars in which you can align your measure of success. For the clients you work with, they will inevitably wrestle with unrealistic expectations surrounding success. Purpose supersedes our culture's definition of success all day, every day. Money, brand recognition, and accolades are not a bad thing. In fact, they are a very good thing. However, those things don't determine your fruitfulness based on the pillars provided within the Purpose Driven Coaching model. Whether you're a professional, an entrepreneur, or both, you have the opportunity to dream dangerous dreams. You are never too late to get your dangerous dream starting. Samuel L. Jackson has starred in multiple movies that have grossed over $2 billion dollars. He has had a long, successful career in Hollywood spanning decades. However, Samuel L. Jackson didn't make his acting breakthrough until he was 40 years old. He got the ball rolling by landing two minor roles for Spike Lee films "School Daze" and "Do the Right Thing" respectively. It is never too late to dream big dreams.

THE CAREER TRINITY

In Purpose Driven Work, I've talked extensively about how values, interests, and skills gave me the context to help me navigate my career. I call these three assessment tools the "Career Trinity." There are so many tools, including Cliftonstrengths, that coaches can use to help themselves and others navigate their careers. I would argue that values, interests, and skills should be the foundation of any career clarity conversation. When you think about values, this relates to how well the aspects of your job fit into the greater theme of your life. When you think about interests, this relates to a person being attracted to a certain type of work. When you think about skills, this relates to how well someone performs a certain type of work.

When it came to Jon Acuff's career, a few of the things he valued included financial stability, career flexibility, and upward mobility. Financial stability was apparent because he could've put all of his eggs in the entrepreneurial basket, but the risk was too high. He needed a career that provided financial stability for his family while making progressive steps over time toward his dream job. He valued career flexibility because, without it, he wouldn't have had the bandwidth to work a day job to take care of his family while investing time in his side hustle. Some careers are rigid and time-consuming. He could have climbed the corporate ladder, but that would have made his opportunity to invest in his side hustle too rigid or restrictive. Lastly, he valued upward mobility, which was evident in his consistent pursuit of his dreams. Some of us don't necessarily want new jobs or new business opportunities in our world of work. Some folks prefer their personal lives to be the arena where adventure and mobility take place. Nothing is wrong with either. Jon wanted more out of his work life, so he blogged and took on side business opportunities because he valued mobility in his professional world.

Martin Eberhard was interested in the world of technology through and through. He was drawn to pursue a degree in the engineering field. From there, his love of technology drew him to create his own eBook. Not settling for economic success, he was drawn to create his own electric vehicle and founded Tesla. Martin has been attracted like a magnet to the world of technology. I'm sure there were plenty of other things that motivated him as a technologist and founder. He could be interested in start-up companies, leading people, problem-solving, and more. With all of these interests being a factor, it is inspiring to see people do amazing things and overcome tremendous challenges by allowing what they like to motivate them.

Skills pay the bills. All of us participate in a workforce that is ever-changing. Companies and institutions are impacted by technology, legislation, the environment, and much more. It took Jon Acuff over ten years to get to his dream job. While he worked his day job, he developed his writing skills, speaking skills, storytelling skills, and an assortment of other skills. It's one thing for us to dream. It is another thing to work towards your dream by growing your skill set. Martin Eberhard and Marc Tarpenning had no clue what it took to create an electric vehicle. By building a prototype, they discovered areas of growth. On the path to creating the most popular automotive company in the United States, the two men learned hundreds of skills, including building battery packs, fundraising, pre-selling, vetting suppliers, coordinating events, and much more. The Career Trinity will provide coaches with the tools to help their clients navigate their careers no matter what industry they work in.

CHAPTER 5

HOME FIELD ADVANTAGE "FINDING YOUR ARENA"

PURPOSE OVER POSITION

It is Fall 2015, and Vad Lee, the starting quarterback for James Madison University, has championship aspirations. The year prior, Vad helped rejuvenate a football program by taking his team to the playoffs for the first time in 2 years. A 2-year playoff hiatus was a huge disappointment for JMU since the fanbase and university experienced deep playoff runs for the greater part of the decade including a National Championship in 2004. Vad had inherited a purpose whether he agreed to it or not. That purpose was to win. This wouldn't be a difficult purpose for Vad to inherit, though. Up until 2015, Vad had spent the greater part of his 22 years on earth cultivating a winning mindset. From Pee Wee, to Pop Warner, to high school, and now college, Vad positioned himself for his purpose. Win.

In 2010, Vad led Hillside High School to its first state championship by leading his team through an undefeated season, going 16 - 0. It was just a few years prior that the Hillside football program had been a laughingstock of the league with a tradition of compiling one losing season after another. From there, Vad went on to attend the Institute of Georgia Tech as a full scholarship student-athlete. The stakes were much higher than in high school, and this was the first time in Vad's life that he realized how important it is to be surrounded by a winning culture, with winning systems, with people that have winning mindsets, and to have the opportunity to win. Vad's first year on campus was as a redshirt. He didn't compete on the field but rather spent the season working out and learning the system. Vad's second year on campus was his redshirt freshman year, where he split time with a senior starter who was the leader of the team, but due to Vad's upside, he contributed in a big way. Even though he didn't get a chance to play as much as he liked, he got an opportunity to help his team in 4 victories, including a victory over Duke where he scored a touchdown. He got a chance to contribute to the success of his team, going 8 - 5 that year, but he still wasn't the primary quarterback. He also didn't compete in a system that was built around his talents, which was the Wing-T Offense. The next year, Vad got a chance to be the starting quarterback. His team finished the year going 7 - 7. Vad got an opportunity to compete, but the circumstances didn't position him to win as he was in an offense that didn't fit his skillset. Vad is athletic, but he is also a passer and a playmaker. The offensive system he was in relegated him to handing the ball off or running. There weren't many opportunities to pass or make plays. In 2014, Vad decided to transfer to James Madison University for a new opportunity. An opportunity to win.

For those of you who might not be a huge football fan or sports fan, I want to share some context about Vad Lee as a person. Vad is what I'd consider an "old soul." When I met him as a transfer student coming from Georgia Tech, it was apparent that he was mature beyond his age. It's possible his "old soul" or spirit of maturity was cultivated from his humble beginnings growing up in the working lower-middle-class community of Durham, North Carolina. It's possible that since he was the black sheep of the family, his faith in Jesus contributed to his mature mindset. It might be possible that the intense workouts and training he'd endured at the hands of his coaches in high school, Georgia Tech, and James Madison contributed to his mental disposition. Regardless of upbringing or which life experiences contributed to his personality, the winning purpose he had adopted hinged more on his eternal perspective of life rather than his athletic endeavors. Up until October 24th, 2015, Vad's position was quarterback, but his position had always been something more than just the work he did. Vad always knew that his winning mindset stemmed from his belief that his purpose was bigger than his position. Purpose over Position.

2 years after leaving Georgia Tech, Vad would lead JMU on a 7 - 0 winning streak. Vad Lee was on the watchlist for the Walter Payton Award as the nation's best FCS offensive player. He was on the watchlist for the FCS National Player of the Year award. NFL draft analysts were projecting him to be drafted between

the 3rd and 7th rounds of that year's draft. His team was picking up major media attention, so much so that ESPN's College GameDay chose James Madison University's homecoming game with the University of Richmond as the host. Just for context, it is rare that an FCS school would get chosen as a host for ESPN's College GameDay. Usually, this is reserved for the likes of major FBS schools such as Alabama, Clemson, Ohio State, and Georgia. The point that I want to make is that Vad was instrumental in the success of the program. As the quarterback of JMU, he positioned himself and the program to win.

In the 3rd quarter of the October 24th homecoming game against the University of Richmond, Vad was leading his team in a game that saw both teams putting up a lot of fireworks. Up to that point, Vad had tossed 2 touchdown passes and ran for 3 touchdowns, accumulating over 400 yards of offense. Looking to give his team the lead with the game tied 35 - 35, Vad rolls out of the pocket to elude pressure from a defender and tosses a 41-yard pass to one of his receivers. The crowd goes wild, as it always does when he makes an electric play. However, all of a sudden, the crowd gets suspiciously quiet as they see Vad hobbling back to the huddle. As Vad gingerly puts pressure on his foot, he gets the call for the next play and communicates the play to his teammates in the huddle. Hoping to give their quarterback a temporary break to let the aches and pain subside, they call a running play where Vad hands the ball to his running back. For three more plays, Vad hands the ball off to his running back until his coach eventually calls a timeout. Never once did Vad think to himself that he should take a knee to the ground so that the trainers could come to his aid. Vad is a winner. He was taught that if you're injured, then you show the mental toughness to stay on your feet and walk to the sideline. That's exactly what Vad did. He walked to the sideline. The trainers assessed his injuries. The trainers told Vad and his coaches that he broke multiple bones in his foot. This would be the end of Vad Lee's college football career.

HOME FIELD ADVANTAGE

As educators, leaders, and workforce development professionals, it is important to create a "Home Field Advantage" for yourself.

Like sports, there are so many factors that are outside of your control. You can't control if the people you serve are going to be receptive to your coaching. You can't control a budget cut that impacts the staffing and resources you now have to work with. Sometimes, you can't control your boss giving you a new initiative that drastically changes the goals and mission of the coaching services you provide. In sports, no matter what perceived disparity in talent levels between competitors, the game can go any way. You can win the game, or you can lose the game. When sports teams play on the road, the odds for victory become increasingly difficult. The crowd isn't on your side. Your daily routine prior to the game looks different. You don't have access to the same resources and facilities that you normally would. Competing at home provides teams with a perceived advantage. For coaches, I want us to adopt a mindset of "Home Field Advantage." With so many elements out of our control, we have to create an environment where things are in our control. We can create a "Home Field Advantage" no matter what the circumstances are.

Ok, Quintrel, that sounds cool and all, but what do you mean? We can learn from Vad's story that no matter what position you're in, there is a purpose in it. Vad's college football career was taken from him in one instant. Vad did experience going through a mourning process as he grieved the abrupt end of his career. But he didn't stay in that position. His purpose always superseded his position. There was a season where his position was that of a college quarterback, but his purpose was to lead his team. His purpose was to minister the gospel of Jesus Christ to people on campus. His purpose was to develop speaking and coaching skills while on campus for future arenas. Vad recounts his story of adversity in his book "Purpose over Position" where he chronicles his football career and the importance of maximizing your calling in every role you're in. As educators, leaders, and workforce development professionals you have a "Home Field Advantage" when you live out your purpose in your position. You have a "Home Field Advantage" when you adopt a winning mindset no matter what external circumstances present themselves. Too many of us become victims because of the circumstances that come our way. Too many of us get stuck in our circumstances because of a defeated mindset rather than changing our perspective or changing our environment. There are four areas that can help you in your role so that you can take "Home Field Advantage," including your reality, your resources, your role, and your roof.

1. **Your Reality.** You have the power to determine the reality of your life. This is about belief. We all have to have faith in something. Your faith determines the reality you live in. If there is never enough money or technology to do a job, then there never will be. However, you can choose a reality that allows you to achieve a desired goal despite the lack of money or technology to complete the goal.

2. **Your Resources.** Sometimes, we do need the necessary resources to accomplish a specific goal. Sometimes, we have to physically retrieve and advocate for the necessary resources to do our work as educators, leaders, and workforce development professionals. Sitting and waiting won't get things done. You will have to find or create the resources needed in order for you to gain a "Home Field Advantage."

3. **Your Role.** When we're trying to accomplish a goal, we must be positioned correctly in order to be fruitful. If you're a coach, then you should understand that your strengths, personality, energy level, and skill set are unique from other coaches. You must position yourself to lean into your giftings in order to be most fruitful. If you're an educator, leader, or workforce development professional, there are a lot of different roles that you can serve to impact organizations. You have to ask yourself, "How am I positioned to achieve the goal I'm called to achieve?"

4. **Your Roof.** All of us need support to do our work, whether that is financial, physical, emotional, spiritual, or something else. We need a person or a group of people to help us do the work we're called to do as educators, leaders, and workforce development professionals. Your roof covers you and protects you from the elements. Positioning yourself under the right roof will allow you to gain a "Home Field Advantage."

Vad's reality was that despite having a career-ending injury, he believed he had a purpose that extended beyond playing quarterback. Because his reality didn't hinge on having success in sports, he was able to position himself as a husband, a father, a motivational speaker, a published author, a sports analyst, a corporate recruiter, and so much more. He knew that being a quarterback was more than just throwing passes to his teammates. His reality told him that being a quarterback was an opportunity to fruitfully impact other people. His reality also reminded him that his athletic career would one day end. Because of that reality, he took the necessary steps to transition from being a quarterback.

While he was at the Institute of Georgia Tech, he realized that he wasn't positioned with the right resources to reach his fullest potential as a quarterback. Despite being a part of a program that had great coaches and facilities, the football systems weren't structured in a way that aligned with his talent. This is especially true for you as educators, leaders, and workforce development professionals. Not only do you have to be self-aware of what you need to succeed, but you'll have to be mindful of helping to position the people you serve with the right resources to succeed.

Vad's role as a quarterback required him to know everyone's position on the field. His role required him to have a comprehensive understanding of the entire offense and not just his job. His role required him to be a vocal leader, to be an encouragement, to align other people with the game plan, and to take command of certain moments. Your role as educators, leaders, and workforce development professionals should align with your strengths and skills. Your role should fulfill you and allow fruitfulness for others. You must know what is required of your role and take complete ownership of that role. The stakes are too high for you to not know what your role is and to not know what to do in it.

With every transition, Vad experienced, whether from high school to Georgia Tech, from Georgia Tech to JMU, or from JMU to the real world, Vad needed a support team around him. There is an old quote that says, "Some people are in your life for the season or the reason." Neither is good or bad. Some folks are going to be in your life for a short time to help you with a specific thing. Some people are going to be ever present in a variety of ways no matter the season simply because of who you are to them. Regardless of the "season or the reason," they are there as your roof. Vad has been surrounded by family, friends, coaches, advisors, administrators, mentors, pastors, supervisors, and much more. When we think about Vad's story, we should ask the question, "Who coached him, and how did coaching impact his life?" The family and friends served as a roof by providing aspects of coaching that filled his emotional and spiritual tank. The sports coaches in his career served as a roof by providing aspects of coaching that equipped him with the technical and physical aspects needed to perform on the field. The advisors and administrators (like myself) served as a roof by providing aspects of coaching that were beyond the athletic field to help make a successful transition after football was over. Vad has a powerful story, but his success wouldn't be possible without people like you to help him. As educators, leaders, and workforce development professionals, you can ensure "Home Field Advantage" by leveraging the people who serve as your "roof."

YOUR UNIQUE DISCONTENT

In the book "Your Purpose is Calling," written by Dr. Dharius Daniels, he unpacks a concept called unique discontent. A person's unique discontent is a problem that they yearn to solve. Many of us have experienced enough frustration in life or have gone through enough trials to give us context about adversity. Through adversity, we come to understand the debts of internal and external factors that make life difficult. As educators, leaders, and workforce development professionals, you face forces that directly compete with your being able to do your job. This year, I conducted training for roughly 50 business partners who provide onsite employment for youth workers. For many of these youths, this was the first time they worked a job. For the employers that supervised the youth, this was their first time supervising. My goal was to provide best practices for how to supervise youth workers and to help the supervisors use their Clifton strengths in the workplace. The supervisors would serve as managers, mentors, and coaches through the youth's employment experience.

Common challenges that these supervisors would face with their youth workers are a lack of professionalism, tardiness and absenteeism, poor customer service, lack of ability to manage workplace conflict, poor communication skills, and much more. Though the opportunity for impact from these supervisors to the youth workers is tremendous, the opportunity can also be extremely frustrating. Many of the supervisors have worked or have come from disadvantaged backgrounds similar to that of the youth. Some of them have discussed how impactful the opportunity will be for these youth to get real-world experience because this could be the experience that opens up doors for their future. For these youth who live in lower-income communities with little opportunity for advancement, the stakes are high, and many of the supervisors know that. Many of the supervisors are motivated by the unique discontent of lack of opportunity for youth in marginalized communities. Though their work experience supervising the youth can be challenging, they are motivated to endure those challenges because of their unique discontent.

As coaches, the stakes are extremely high in the arena that you serve. Many of your clients will provide a challenge to you that will be difficult to endure. Some of the challenges you might encounter are interpersonal, cultural, organizational, community-related, institutional, or systemic. Despite what might seem like insurmountable odds at times; your unique discontent as a coach will be the catalyst that allows you to endure. Your unique discontent should motivate you to think outside the box. It should force you to be creative. It should force you to use emotional intelligence. Your unique discontent should force you to develop the mental fortitude to produce fruitfulness in your arena.

In "Purpose Driven Work," I talked about my motivation to transition from being a Sports Performance Coach to an Academic Advisor. I always enjoyed working in the collegiate athletic environment. Being around athletes, competition, and the facilities always felt like a familiar place to me. As a Sports

Performance Coach, I'd develop comprehensive exercise programs to help my athletes with their physical attributes to perform in their respective sports. Though I enjoyed this work, I felt as though my impact was limited. I wanted to have an impact on people that transcended what they did on the field but also translated to what they would do when they could no longer compete on the field. I decided that I wanted to be an Academic Advisor for student-athletes because many of the young adults who came to college had no clue what they could do beyond their sport. I remember having college teammates and peers finish school and go back to the lower socio-economic communities that they grew up in. I saw teammates who got into legal trouble that landed them in jail or probation. I saw countless teammates who picked up alcohol and drug habits that put them on a path of self-destruction. Most of these student-athletes had a four-year degree and four years of work experience as a student-athlete but had no clue how to translate that into the workforce. This was my unique discontent. This problem was the motivator for me to transition into being an Academic Advisor. This unique discontent is what has propelled me as a coach, facilitator, speaker, author, and storyteller. Sometimes, the work has been thankless. I've nudged and challenged student-athletes to invest in their lives beyond the field to the point where they didn't like me. Because I cared more about their success beyond sports, I've been disrespected and name-called by some of them. What allowed me to endure is my unique discontent to help transform mindsets, spark dreams, and coach folks on their path beyond sports.

USING IKIGAI FOR LANGUAGE AND VISUAL

Language and visual illustration are some of the most powerful tools when it comes to providing clarity to people. Many of us coaches have stumbled into this type of work because we simply want to help others but just don't know how to do it. As educators, leaders, and workforce development professionals, there are so many things you do in your world of work. Your attention, efforts, and energy are most of the time divided by organizational demands. Rarely does it seem like you have the opportunity to fully clarify the arena you'd like to serve or help clarify what arenas the people you help should serve in. Ikigai provides language and a visual illustration that can be helpful for you and your clients.

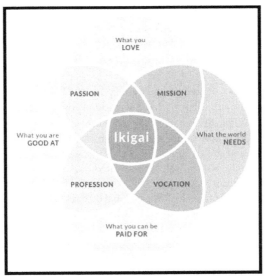

Figure 5.1 is the Ikigai illustration.

Ikigai has been prescribed as a tool to find the purpose of life, happiness in life, holistic health, operating in flow, a tool for longevity, and much more. I'm not here to introduce Ikigai to any of these ideas. The Purpose Driven Coaching model isn't meant to be a tool to help you find purpose in life either. The PDC model is meant to help you align purpose with the work that you do as educators, leaders, and workforce development. You can find your purpose by asking God yourself and reading about it in His word. With Ikigai, the illustration provides a way for you to negotiate things such as your passion, your mission, your professional work, your skills, your personal desires, and what you can get compensated for. In certain seasons, you may want to prioritize doing work you're good at with work opportunities you'll be appropriately compensated for. In other seasons you may want to clarify what it is that you love to do and invest as much time as possible towards figuring that out. I see Ikigai as a tool where I can ask myself "what matters most" to help provide a path of clarity. Common Ikigai-related questions I'd ask my client would be:

- What things are you good at that you can be fairly compensated for in your career?
- What do you think the world needs, and in what way can you serve that need?
- How does your business align with your personal mission?
- Who are people you look up to who love what they do and are solving what the world needs?
- What can you be paid if you were to do what you're good at in your career vs. your own business?

If you were to ask yourself Ikigai-related questions for your career or entrepreneurial journey, you'd be bound to keep "Home Field Advantage." We all have different desires and needs as the seasons change, and when those seasons do change, you can maintain your spot in the arena by using Ikigai as a tool for reflection and clarity.

COMPETING IN MY ARENA

I use a lot of sports references in my writing because my journey in the workforce began in an athletic environment. As an athlete, then as a Sports Performance Coach, and then as an Academic Advisor within college athletics, there is simply no way I'd be where I am professionally without sports. In high school, we adopted a tradition that I later found out was borrowed from the old-school Notre Dame football program. As we walked outside our locker room door towards the field, there was a sign that said, "Play like a champion today." Every one of us would tap the sign as we left the locker room. The practice became second nature to us that even if we did have a game or practice and were leaving the locker room, we'd impulsively slap the sign. For us, it set a mental expectation that I'm going into the arena to do work. As educators, leaders, and workforce development professionals, there should be a deep mindset you adopt that as you're entering your arena, you're going to do championship-caliber work. As you hop out of your car and walk into your place of business, you're walking into an arena. As you open your laptop to hop on a Zoom call with a client, you're logging into a virtual arena. You're about to play like a champion.

COACHING IS NOT MY PRIMARY ROLE

In our arenas, some of us won't serve as a coach in our primary role. If you're an educator, leader, or workforce development professional, you must understand who your clients are, how to balance administration, how to balance other roles, and how to incorporate strategic planning in your role. All of us have clients, no matter what our role is. If you're a manager who supervises a team of employees, then they are your clients. If you are an associate or a specialist who doesn't have anyone you supervise, then your clients are your cross-functional teammates. If you are an entrepreneur that partners with organizations, then you're coaching the key stakeholders that you partner with. All of us have clients. Consider the PDC model in which there are four pillars of purpose that we contribute to, including individual, population, territorial expansion, and territorial control. You will provide coaching to the folks you serve with the consideration of those four pillars. As coaches, we can critique our coaching practices by asking:

- Am I coaching in a way that is physically, mentally, emotionally, and spiritually fruitful for me?
- Am I coaching in a way that helps others to be physically, mentally, emotionally, and spiritually fruitful?
- Am I coaching in a way that helps people perform better in the workplace?
- Am I coaching in a way that contributes to the success and sustainability of the organizations I serve?

Balancing the administrative aspects of your role will position you to maximize your coaching opportunities. With consideration to strengths, some of us are talented at executing, influencing others, building relationships, or strategic thinking. Knowing the areas you are stronger in will allow you to tackle the administrative aspects strategically. For those of us who are not administratively oriented, we can adopt a mindset that intentionally leverages our Clifton strengths to tackle the administrative aspects of our role. Whether it is a matter of time management, project management, or preference, if we own the administrative aspects of our role, we can be confident that this will contribute to us better serving our clients.

If coaching isn't the primary part of your role and you're in a position where you have to wear multiple hats, then you will likely have to be intentional about creating coaching opportunities. Most of us will serve in a middle management role as associates or specialists, which means we'll constantly have to negotiate multiple projects in our jobs. Your clients can be your colleagues, direct reports, customers, external vendors, and much more. Balancing other roles will require coaching to be most effective if it isn't left to happenstance. Keep in mind that coaching is a social contract that usually takes place for a duration of time. There is a level of expectation that is built into the coaching experience. Educators, leaders, and workforce development professionals can plan coaching conversations ahead in order to help juggle multiple roles. They can foster developmental coaching by nudging their clients to take ownership of setting up days and times to meet. This may alleviate an administrative burden for the coach. Balancing other roles will require individuals to be strategic and creative.

Strategic planning is critical for individuals who provide coaching but also have other roles within their job function. Not only should they be strategic about balancing their role to determine how coaching fits in, but they should also zoom out to be strategic with the people that they serve. If you plan on having a program or cohort-like strategy to serve large amounts of clients, then you'll need to assess the needs of those folks collectively. There will be some planning that needs to take place in order to consider the goals, best methods, the content to be shared, coaching questions, and more. At Lenore Coaching LLC, we implement our Momentum program with multiple business partners, which can range from 10 clients to over 100 clients at a time. The program stays fairly consistent for each group; however, we take a lot of time to plan out how each program will be implemented. There are always subtle changes that make a huge difference in engagement for each group of clients we serve.

COACHING IS MY PRIMARY ROLE

Even if coaching isn't your primary role, the details discussed in this section should be things to consider when you do provide coaching. If coaching is your primary focus, like every profession, you should be a lifelong learner. Coaching is both an art and a science, so there are always ways to improve as a coach. The PDC model isn't meant to prescribe purpose for you, but as a coach, it will be a continual process to align your purpose with the work that you do. There are five ideas to consider as coaches, including your niche, the medium, your style, and cultural awareness.

Your niche is your area of specialty within the coaching field. As industries evolve, the areas for coaching will evolve; however, some common niches you can consider for educators, leaders, and workforce development professionals include:

- Career Coaching
- Leadership Coaching
- Executive Coaching
- Performance or Success Coaching
- Conflict Coaching
- Sales Coaching
- Transformational Coaching

Your niche should be an area where you're naturally drawn towards and have the capacity to build skills. For many individuals, the importance of finding a niche is to have a depth of knowledge and skills for the purpose of providing value to the people you serve. Many professionals may serve as generalists until they themselves or the organizations they serve see a need for a greater focus in a specific niche. Having a niche doesn't mean that you can't continue to grow in other areas of coaching or the workforce. Rather, having a niche speaks to seeing the value of helping to solve specific problems with people or for organizations. For the first part of my career, I served as a generalist with a broad knowledge of how to help individuals in the education space. My interests would later draw me to specialize in career and workforce development. The roles I served in were coaching-specific roles. As my career progressed, I was nudged by organizations to enhance my skill set, which ultimately afforded me the opportunity to develop a niche in career coaching.

The medium as a coach is the areas where you will physically engage with your clients. The medium doesn't have to be one size fits all when you serve clients. Examples of medium include but are not limited to:

- In-Person
- Synchronous Virtual
- Asynchronous Virtual
- Individual
- Group

Technology will continue to innovate, and organizations will continue to change, so the possibilities for mediums that coaches engage their clients will continue to change. As coaches, we have to assess the best circumstances to deliver coaching based on the client's needs and the situation. If our clients have a skill gap with utilizing technology, then coaches need to provide training or switch the medium. If there are some conversations that have an intimate topic, then it may be more appropriate to meet in person. If you've been contracted to serve hundreds of clients, then it might not be realistic to meet with them individually. Coaches should get comfortable and develop the skills needed to provide quality coaching in the mediums of choice.

Your style of coaching should be reflected through the combination of your client's needs, your Clifton strengths, your coaching skills, your personality, cultural knowledge and cultural awareness, and the medium. Coaches should work their hardest to be their authentic selves. It isn't easy being your most authentic self, though. What might sound easy actually takes years of practice. A state of "flow" is often evidence that coaches have found their coaching style. Flowstate occurs when conversations seem natural, and coaches have confidence in their abilities. Clients may have certain expectations or preferences with their coaches, such as space to talk, engaging body language, directness, open-mindedness, intrusive, developmental, and much more. Coaches shouldn't have to change who they are as a person but rather show an ability to sense how a client is feeling and respond accordingly. Your skill set as a coach should constantly progress. Depending on where you are in your career, your coaching style will reflect the skills in your toolkit. Your personality is a reflection of your coaching style, which might range from extraversion to introversion, gentle to assertive, imaginative to process-oriented, and everything in between. Be authentic while being mindful of how your personality will impact the coaching experience with your clients. There are plenty of times when you can flex up or scale back on some of your personality traits. Similar to personality, using your Strengths allows coaches to create the ideal experiences for their clients. You have the power to greatly influence the coaching experience with consideration to how you use your talents within the four themes of Execution, Influencing, Relationship Building, and Strategic Thinking. Lastly, our communities and the workforce consist of diverse people from all types of backgrounds, including ethnicities, sex, gender, religion, socio-economic, and much more. Coaches should expand their cultural knowledge to lead equitable and inclusive coaching conversations.

Cultural awareness includes being conscious of organizational culture and its implications for policy, practice, teaching, research, and community engagement. Bias can happen consciously and unconsciously, which can greatly affect the nature of the coach and client relationship. Conscious bias, in its extreme, is characterized by overt negative behavior that can be expressed through physical and verbal harassment or through more subtle means such as exclusion. For example, conscious bias knowingly occurs when someone makes a negative comment about another person because of that person's ethnic or racial identity. Conscious bias can occur if a person perpetuates a stereotype about another person. For example, if a coach makes a comment to a female client to lean into her natural nurturing attributes as a woman when leading, that would perpetuate a stereotype. Unconscious bias operates outside of the person's awareness and can be in direct contradiction to a person's espoused beliefs and values. For example, if a career coach is helping a white male to clarify their career goals and subconsciously is guiding him towards progressing into a leadership role, that would be an example of unconscious bias. Cultural awareness is critical for coaches in order to minimize bias, stereotypes, and any practices that prevent an equitable and inclusive space for the client.

As educators, leaders, and workforce development professionals, your ability to effectively coach has the potential to transform lives. Your coaching ability allows individuals to perform at a top level within the workforce. Your role as a coach can help others to align purpose effectively within the four pillars of the Purpose Driven Coaching model. "Home Field Advantage" is something that coaches will have to work hard in order to attain. Like athletes preparing to go into hostile territories with factors beyond their control, coaches can embrace a mindset that allows them to regain the advantage no matter what comes their way. That mindset is a winning mindset, a resilient mindset, and one that is growth-oriented. Whether coaching is or isn't a primary part of your role, your arena provides coaching opportunities to make a fruitful impact.

CHAPTER 6

TACKLING WORKFORCE CHALLENGES

THE INTERCONNECTION BETWEEN SOCIETY CHALLENGES & THE WORKFORCE (PART 1)

Joe Hernandez from NPR writes, "The financial giant Lehman Brothers filed for bankruptcy on Sept. 15, 2008, with $613 billion in debt, putting thousands of employees out of work and sending the already recessionary economy into a tailspin. The dramatic fall of Lehman was due in large part to millions of risky mortgages propping up an unstable financial system. Homebuyers with mortgage payments they couldn't afford defaulted on their loans, sending shockwaves through Wall Street and leaving those borrowers vulnerable to foreclosure."

- Where did those people go to work after they were laid off?
- How did the hit on their confidence and mental health impact their job search process?
- What other industries were negatively impacted by the housing crisis?

In response to A.I.'s impact on jobs, Greg Iacurci from CNBC writes, 'The high exposure group includes occupations like budget analysts, data entry keyers, tax preparers, technical writers and web developers. They often require more analytical skills, and A.I. may, therefore, replace or assist their "most important" job functions...Technology makes some workers more productive. That reduces costs and prices for goods and services, leading consumers to "feel richer" and spend more, which fuels new job creation..."

- What industries will grow or decrease because of A.I.?
- How will A.I. impact the disparity of wealth?
- A.I. will directly increase consumerism, so how will this impact the environment?

A Forbes article written by Mark C. Perna explains, "For two years now, America's teachers have coped with virtual/hybrid pandemic school, Covid-19 learning slide, societal unrest, and deep political polarities, alongside their own personal challenges. As a result, a significant number are about to call it quits and leave the profession for good. Education is heading for a crisis of epic proportions—and in many places, it's already started."

- How will legislation play a role in addressing teacher shortages?
- In what ways will teachers leaving the profession impact college education programs and processes to attract prospective teachers?
- How can career coaches help educators to rebrand and re-skill for new employment opportunities?

Research by the Urban Institute Initiative states, "Over the past few years, the COVID-19 pandemic, record-high inflation, significant job losses, and rising rent prices have shaped the affordable housing landscape. Between 2019 and 2021, the shortage of homes affordable and available to renters with extremely low incomes worsened by more than 500,000 units, increasing from a shortage of 6.8 million to 7.3 million, and continuing a long-term trend of diminishing supply. Addressing the shortage of affordable and available housing is vital to ensuring families across the U.S. experience financial security, improved health, educational opportunities, and greater economic mobility."

- How does affordability in the housing market impact the career decisions employees make, and how does that impact the available workforce in specific industries?
- What relationship does racial and cultural conflict have with the housing market demand?
- There is a proliferation of economic disparity between black and white communities perpetuated in part by the housing market, but in what ways do talent shortages improve the issue?

Kathryn Watson from CBS News writes, "The Biden administration's announcement that up to $20,000 in student loan debt will be canceled for borrowers will bring welcome relief to millions, as long as courts allow. But that relief won't do anything to slow the rapidly rising cost of going to college. If the published cost of the college remained in line with inflation, annual tuition and fees would have been $2,076 at four-year public universities and $8,624 at private institutions for the 2020-2021 academic year, according to the National Center for Education Statistics data in constant dollars, or income adjusted for inflation. But in the 2020-2021 academic year, the average price tag for in-state tuition and fees at a four-year public institution was $9,375, and at private four-year institutions, it was a whopping $32,825. With student housing, that cost skyrockets — some schools are charging those who can afford it over $70,000 per year."

- How does the cost of education contribute to bi-partisan political polarization?
- Company culture is arguably impacted by labor shortages, but in what way are labor shortages impacted by the cost of education?
- In what ways can technology positively influence the cost of education?

An article from Harvard Business Review highlights, "The impact of work from home on energy use is mixed, with some studies finding a positive effect, while others indicating a neutral or even a negative impact on energy use. Ultimately, such impacts can vary substantially by employee's individual characteristics (e.g., awareness, attitudes, family size, wealth), home infrastructure (e.g., building energy ratings, supplier), and even situational factors (e.g., geographic location and season). When companies craft remote work policies, for instance, by subsidizing home energy bills, they also need to account for sustainability impacts from residential energy emissions. From an individual footprint perspective, our digital behaviors add up. One study suggests that a "typical business" user — albeit in the pre-Covid-19 period — creates 135kg (298lbs) CO_2e (i.e., carbon dioxide equivalent) from sending emails every year, which is the equivalent of driving 200 miles in a family car, just under the distance from Brussels to London.

- How have work-from-home policies impacted the housing market?
- How will federal legislation to address environmental sustainability impact profitability for organizations?
- How can education institutions address skills gaps associated with work-from-home policies?

THE INTERCONNECTION BETWEEN SOCIETY CHALLENGES & THE WORKFORCE (PART 2)

Tina Turner's classic 1984 hit "What's Love Got to Do With It" embodies the interconnection between systems. The song is about love. It's not about her being in love but rather her assessment of what people perceive it to be like when they are in love. She sings, *"You must understand, though the touch of your hand makes my pulse react. It's only the thrill of a boy meeting a girl; opposites attract. It's physical. Only logical. You must try to ignore that it means more than that."* Straight out of the gates, there is an exuberance that each of us feels when we first meet someone. When we first see, talk, and touch someone we're attracted to, it can be an exciting feeling to have. Tina Turner is calling that out. In a direct but subtle way, she undermines the feeling by saying, "Hey, look, brother man or sister girl, this person might seem like they are all that and a bag of chips at this moment, but understand it's just attraction."

I believe the heart of the song is telling listeners that there is more to love than what our senses are telling us. I think she is trying to get us to look at love in the context of how two people relate to one another. I think she's nudging us to think about the health of a relationship and the plethora of things that go into making a relationship healthy and sustainable. I think she's charging us to go beyond the feelings of euphoria and excitement that attracted people towards one another and challenging us to love in the context of a truly harmonious relationship. If I were you, I'd definitely be asking myself, "Where is this brother going with this Tina Turner song, and what does it have to do with coaching?" To that, I'd like to compare our workforce to Tina Turner's definition of love, which is about a sustainable and healthy relationship between two people that have many dimensions they bring into that relationship, including personality, background, beliefs, and much more. Love has its challenges. The workforce has its challenges. With love, there is an interconnection between people. With the workforce there is an interconnection between people, organizations with people in them, and systems which ultimately consist of even larger bunches of people. With love, there are a lot of things below the surface that play a big role.

With the workforce, there are a lot of things below the surface that play a big role. From Chapter 5, we've learned that the niches coaches can serve include career coaching, leadership coaching, executive coaching, performance coaching, conflict coaching, sales coaching, transformational coaching, and much more. In these niches, we play a small role in macro-level impact in the workforce. As coaches, we are the ones getting underneath the surface to play a big role. As coaches, we're the ones who are interconnected with each other and the folks we serve who make up our organizations and systems. Like love, the workforce has its challenges, and as coaches, we're the ones at the tip of the spear, attacking those challenges head-on.

PROVIDING VALUE TO DIFFERENT PARTS OF AN ORGANIZATION

At this point, my hope is that you understand that you are a coach no matter what role you play in an organization, whether you are an educator, leader, or workforce development professional. For those of you who are independent coaches running your own business, you will often work directly with a client population who serve in different areas of an organization. Regardless of who your clients are and what your relationship is with an organization, it is important to understand the hierarchy of an organization. Doing so will allow you to understand who your primary clients are within the company and how to prioritize the right goals with that person.

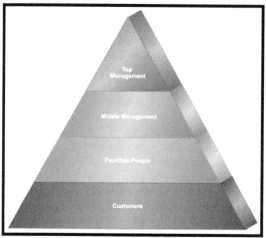

Figure 6.1 is an illustration of the traditional organizational pyramid

In Figure 6.1, we can see the traditional hierarchy of an organization, starting from bottom to top, including the customer, the frontline people, middle management, and then top management. **The customer is the recipient of the product or service that the organization provides.** Without the customer, the organization will not be able to sustain itself. Customers are critical because they also give the organization feedback on their needs. If an organization doesn't strategically address the needs of the customer, then it risks losing them, which in turn displaces the organization's share in a competitive market. The data and feedback from customers are critical information to the people who work for the organization in some shape or fashion.

The frontline people are those individuals who provide the product or service to the customer or someone who provides the most direct value to customers. Frontline workers drastically impact the customer experience. High-performing Frontline employees often impact customer retention and customer satisfaction more than the actual product or service. Companies invest most of their time and money in improving performance challenges in their organizations with

Frontline employees. This can range from sales coaching, customer service training, leadership development programs, and more. As a coach, you will often have to help Frontline employees understand how important their role is to the customer and the sustainability of the organization. Clarifying how high the stakes are for Frontline employees may help give them the necessary motivation so that performance can improve. Coaching questions you might ask Frontline employees include but are not limited to:

- How can I help you?
- Why are we doing it this way?
- In what ways do you see us living our company values?
- What are common concerns that customers have?
- What are ways that your manager can help you?
- What motivates you?
- How are your strengths being used?
- How does this role help with your future?

Middle managers control organizational "drift," pass information up and down the chain and provide coaching to Frontline employees. Middle managers are in a very difficult position as they are the employees who face pressure from the bottom and top of the organization. Often, they are the ones who serve as advocates and have to vocalize pain points on behalf of Frontline employees surrounding the customer experience. Middle managers who have support from their supervisors are usually positioned to succeed. However, Middle managers also face pressure from Top management about new initiatives, performance concerns, customer feedback, and more. Organizational culture is critical to retaining top Middle manager talent since they are the ones who most impact culture and perpetuate culture. Organizational "drift" is normal for all organizations. Drift occurs naturally when the mission or goals become slowly disconnected from the products or services the company offers. This indirectly impacts the attitudes and behaviors of staff, which can ultimately contribute to drift. Middle managers are the ones who constantly align organizational goals with the people who execute those goals. Healthy drift and changes occur when Middle managers are able to pass Frontline employee and customer information up the chain so that Top management can make strategic decisions. For example, if customers provide feedback to Frontline employees that they want crispier French Fries, then Middle managers will build a business case to Top management about enhancing fry-making processes because of the customer data they've received. When Top management approves the plan and allocates money and resources to enhance the fry-making processes, it will hinge on Middle managers to implement the new processes, which ultimately improve the quality of French Fry for the customer. There are plenty of coaching opportunities to serve Middle managers within an organization. Coaches might ask some of the following questions:

- What challenges are you facing?
- How have priorities been competing with one another, and what has been your approach?
- What is most useful or valuable to you?
- Where are the common bottlenecks in your work?
- What skills are you commonly using to get your work done?
- What are some areas where you need improvement?
- How can your manager or direct reports best help you?
- In what ways are you hoping for a coach to help you?

Top management or executives oversee the operations, finances, and general direction of a business, corporation, or organization. Top management is responsible for leading and sustaining the overall organization. When you zoom out and look at where the company is positioned in the market, Top management has to navigate the forces that keep a company from being successful. Top management has to steward company resources and talent strategically. Top management will make financial decisions or investments to help retain or expand the organization's position in the market. For a nonprofit workforce development organization, Top management may have to steward philanthropic contributions and state funding to prioritize costs associated with programming, staffing, facilities, technology, and more. The nonprofit organization might not generate revenue, so Top management will have to invest efforts towards fundraising and grant writing in order to keep the organization financially sustainable. While sustainability is important, Top management is also the culture setter for the organization. They are the ones who establish and champion the values they wish the organization to have. Top management should constantly exemplify a positive culture but also get feedback from various parts of the organization about the culture. Hiring talented individuals, developing leaders, and building trust at all levels is critical for a healthy organizational culture. Coaching questions for Top management include but are not limited to:

- What are your biggest accomplishments?
- What are your biggest challenges?
- What resources do you need to do your job?
- In what ways are you running the company, and in what ways are you leading it?
- If you were to put your employees into two categories, do you have more participants or contributors?
- What is the vision of the organization?
- How has the organization changed over time?
- What areas could a coach help you to succeed?

USING PESTLE ANALYSIS AS A COACH

Organizations are vulnerable to change because of the people that work in them. Each person in a company reflects and impacts the culture, the mission, the delivery of the product or service, and the customer experience. Since each person has the potential to change various parts of the organization, each person should be equipped with the tools and frameworks to do so strategically. As a coach, your role is to help individuals in the organization to analyze problems and solve them strategically. I like the "3 Roles" phrase for coaches, which says, "Your role is to help people know their role and play their role in the organization." In other words, coaches should help individuals analyze the value chain of a company and then strategically provide value to those areas.

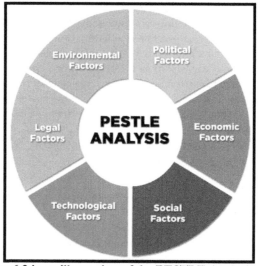

Figure 6.2 is an illustration of the PESTLE Analysis cycle

Figure 6.2 illustrates the PESTLE analysis diagram, which includes political, economic, social, technological, legal, and environmental. Human Resource professionals and Executives use the PESTLE analysis diagram to do an environmental scan of the forces that impact the organization. For example, a new law mandating local municipalities to fund $50,000,000 annually towards youth workforce initiatives will directly impact programming and staffing for city government agencies. Each one of those pillars in the diagram influences the organization. Coaches can use the PESTLE analysis tool to contextualize how their clients' role impacts the organization. Coaches can use this tool proactively for change management scenarios to help Top management executives. Coaches can do exercises with Middle managers and Frontline employees to enhance performance in certain areas. A great skill that coaches can use is the ability to tell a story. Storytelling allows the coach to help their clients gain better perspective so the client ultimately takes ownership to improve their performance.

In my day job, I work for a nonprofit Education Technology Workforce Development organization that provides career readiness services to help underserved populations break into the tech industry. The primary service we provide is coaching, large group facilitation, and resource sharing. One of the individuals I supervise is extremely talented when it comes to ideas and problem-solving. This person will often help teammates to think outside the box to provide value to their clients. This person rarely has a shortage of ideas and best practices that could potentially help teammates with their clients. One of the challenges this person runs into is spending an excessive amount of time collecting ideas, researching ideas, and overcommitting themselves to exciting new initiatives for cross-functional projects. The primary responsibility that this person and their teammates have is to manage a caseload of clients. As their supervisor, this person has been vocal with me about feeling overwhelmed at times when it comes to managing multiple caseloads of clients they have. As their supervisor, I used coaching skills to get to the root cause and help them take ownership of solving their problems. I used the PESTLE analysis tool as a baseline to tell them a story relating to prioritizing their efforts. I told them how the organization has recently received a multi-million dollar donation from an anonymous donor for the organization's mission and footprint to expand. The organization currently serves roughly 5,000 clients each year, and this donation would allow the company to double that footprint. Given that this person was struggling to manage their current caseload of clients and the possibility of our team having to double the number of clients, this story began to help them see how they needed to prioritize their efforts. We continued to have coaching conversations about best practices and skills surrounding caseload management, but by contextualizing PESTLE into a story, this person was able to begin owning their problem. Keep in mind that the goal of a coach isn't to solve their client's problems but to create an atmosphere where their clients can solve their own problems.

MICRO TO MACRO IMPACT AS COACHES

The PESTLE analysis diagram allows educators, leaders, and workforce development professionals to get a big-picture view of how the organization is influenced by external factors. Many of us can get lost in our own little worlds and lose focus on how our work connects to something greater. Often, coaches will have to help these insulated folks zoom out and gain perspective so they can make a change. Many of us have the opposite challenge where we're such a big picture that it might be frustrating to know that you play a small role, knowing there are such great challenges out there. For these folks, coaches will have to ground them and help them understand that there is importance in doing the simple and basic things within our roles to make an impact. No matter how insulated we have a tendency to be or how minuscule we perceive our impact to be, I would offer a "Micro to Macro" perspective in our roles as coaches. When we align the work we do with the Purpose Driven Coaching model, we will inevitably have a macro-level impact. The strength in macro-level impact lies in our ability to partner congruently with others on the same mission. The strength for large-scale impact doesn't come through being fruitful in the individual pillar of the PDC model, but rather the last three pillars: population, territorial expansion, and territorial control. However, without micro-level impact, we can't have macro-level impact. The micro-level impact is all about you being individually fruitful in your world of work. If you don't invest the knowledge, skills, and grow in confidence that is individually fruitful for you, then it is unlikely that you will have a macro-level impact. Notice I said "unlikely" rather than impossible!

In Chapter 2, I offered the metaphor of a tightrope walker to understand the Purpose Driven Coaching model. With constant tension on the rope, multiple forces have to be negotiated in order for that person to walk purposefully across the rope. The PDC model is meant to be a tool to help people clarify how they align purpose with the work they do. The forces that coaches may have to negotiate could be expectations from clients, lack of resources to perform their work, ethical dilemmas contrasted with contractual obligations, self-confidence, skill gaps, and more. When it comes to coaches being individually fruitful they are developing their "why". Individual fruitfulness for a coach relates to the coach developing the knowledge, skills, and confidence in themselves. With practice and feedback, coaches become individually fruitful in their world of work. The cool thing about this idea is that we can see the interdependency of other people with our growth and development. A coach will often have to coach you in order to help you be individually fruitful. Inversely, they are showing population fruitfulness. The work we do with others as coaches is an example of population fruitfulness. Territorial expansion and control will require highly skilled people working highly collaborative. The emphasis on individual fruitfulness is to increase the attributes needed for us to perform, while population fruitfulness emphasizes helping others increase their attributes needed to perform. Territorial expansion is when population fruitfulness happens at scale. Figure 6.3 provides a visual illustration of our roles as coaches throughout the PDC model.

Figure 6.3 is an illustration of a tightrope walker within the PDC model

In Figure 6.3, you can see the person by themself as they negotiate a variety of forces as they walk their own tightrope. This first pillar should help us to analyze how we're growing on our own journey. When we look back in time, do we see progress in certain areas as coaches? Do we see positive patterns or negative patterns? In Figure 6.3, we can look at the population pillar and see someone walking the tightrope while there is someone standing behind them as a coach. The coach in the picture is you. You are now in a position where you are the person helping others to walk their tightrope. Just as there may have been a coach or tribe of coaches that helped you to be individually fruitful, you're now in a position to help others to be individually fruitful. You should analyze your progress in this pillar through the lens of other people's fruitfulness. As a coach, are people showing signs of growth? Do they give you feedback about how you've helped them? Are you able to see positive patterns in the people you coach? I caution you to understand that your purpose isn't determined by someone else's fruitfulness, but rather, your performance in the population pillar is evident by the fruitfulness of the people you serve. If you can recall Vad Lee's mantra in Chapter 5, that your purpose is bigger than your position. Purpose over Position!

Looking at the illustration Figure 6.3, territorial expansion shows multiple people walking a tightrope with an airplane next to them. The airplane is a symbol for expanding to a new place. The multiple tightrope walkers represent you in partnership with other educators, leaders, and workforce development professionals on the same mission. The people you partner with can be in the same business unit, same organization, same region, and more. These folks can also be loosely affiliated from an organizational perspective. For example, your personal mission may be focused on giving equitable access to career opportunities to folks living in underserved communities. You might not have anyone on your team or organization that does the work or shares the same mission as you. Instead, your tribe of people might be affiliated with regional or national professional organizations. Your partners can be loosely associated in terms of day-to-day projects and organizations. But what does it mean to expand territories? Simply put, the work you do as a coach helps to grow organizations, institutions, and geographies. Growth can be difficult to measure, but it should be centered around the fruitfulness of people. We can pass new laws, contribute economically, and provide education, but at the end of the day, are people more fruitful in the way that God intended? This is really difficult to wrestle with and sometimes hard to measure through the lens of companies. Often, our companies don't have a mission that aligns with the PDC model. That is perfectly okay. You should know that your collaboration with people and contributions as a coach are not married to businesses. Alignment of your purpose has eternal implications rather than perspectives associated with brick and mortar.

Lastly, if territorial expansion is about multiplication, then territorial control is about sustainability. Many Fortune 500 companies have missions, policies, values, and OKRs around sustainability now because they know how difficult it is to stay in business. Companies that existed 100 years ago had customers who may have felt like the business was everlasting, but now those businesses are a figment of our imagination. Rest in peace to all of the malls many of us spent our teenage years frolicking in. In Figure 6.3, territorial control is represented with a globe that symbolizes the location you and your collaborators inhabit. Territorial control takes constant work and alignment with those that are adjacent to you on your mission.

CHAPTER 7

TACKLING CAREER READINESS AND WORKFORCE CHALLENGES IN OUR EDUCATION SYSTEMS

WORKFORCE CHALLENGES AT HAND

If you made it to this point in the book, I hope that you have begun to gain clarity on your role as a coach or how to use coaching in your role. My hope is that your ultimate measure of success is determined by how you align purpose with the work that you do. James 2:17 (NLT) says, ***"Faith without works is dead."*** Regardless of what your faith or religious affiliation is, I think it is generally understood by many of us that just saying you believe something isn't enough. Merely hoping and wishing for something in life to be better is one thing. Most of us have come to realize that it takes action to get things accomplished. We can dream up the biggest dream for our lives, organizations, and communities that we want, but ultimately, we're going to have to take action in order to see that dream become reality. Coaching is a vehicle to make dreams become realities.

The unfortunate reality of our workforce is there are some huge challenges for professionals and organizations. 63% of recruiters say there aren't enough qualified candidates for the positions they are sourcing. 69% of human resources professionals surveyed said there is a skills gap in the organizations they work for. What's interesting is that when organizations are able to get qualified talent in the door, there are still cultural difficulties in regard to diversity and generational differences in the workplace. An article by CNBC said, *"Gen Z are digital natives, and they've always communicated online, so their interpersonal skills, or soft skills, have suffered"* in regards to older and younger generations working together in the workplace. Underwhelming feedback was provided from workers in a study by the Pew Research Center regarding diversity, equity, and inclusion in the workplace, saying, *"Relatively small shares of workers place a lot of importance on diversity at their workplace. About three in ten say it is extremely or very important to them to work somewhere with a mix of employees of different races and ethnicities."* These perspectives provide a frustrating but honest picture of our reality. We have a long way to go and a lot of work to do.

Finding qualified talent has not been a new challenge for organizations. At the time of my writing this book in Fall 2023, there are just under 9 million available jobs in the workforce. What's interesting is that there are currently just over 6 million unemployed workers in the U.S. Hypothetically, if every one of those unemployed workers found a job, there would still be over 2 million open jobs in the market. Obviously, if the answer was as easy as just finding those people and giving them a job, then our problems would be solved. However, that is not the case. The employment gap is a very nuanced challenge in our workforce. The reality is that even before the Covid-19 global pandemic, workforce gaps were apparent. Long before "The Great Resignation" and "The Great Reshuffle" were popularized on social media and became a rotational talking point in articles and news segments, people were exiting the workforce at exceptional rates. The reasons why people were leaving corporate America or changing jobs make our workforce challenges difficult to fully understand. Going back to the Fall of 2021, nearly 50% of workforce exits were due to professionals retiring. It is unclear what pre and post-pandemic variables nudged folks into retirement, but it should be noted that the demographics are uniform across the board for which individuals are retiring. Research shows that the nearly 3 million workers who are retiring are mostly white and college-educated individuals. The Bureau of Labor Statistics projects that between 2020 and 2030, there will be a 40% increase in 65 to 69-year-olds being in the labor force by 2030, up from 33% in 2020. This points to the fact that workforce participation is interconnected with greater societal challenges and inequities such as cost of living, childcare, transportation, housing, education, and more.

For example, lack of access to affordable childcare is a major contributing factor to a decrease in workforce participation. Many professionals have found it increasingly difficult to afford childcare and have also found it difficult to manage a household as working parents. It's one thing for people to struggle with the financial burden associated with finding childcare providers for their families, but it is a whole different challenge for working parents to cope with work-related stress while having a family. Certainly, men are leaving the workforce because of childcare challenges, but by and large, women are leaving the workforce at greater rates when it comes to affordable childcare. In the spring of 2020, nearly 3.5 million mothers left their jobs, which drove workforce participation for working mothers from 70% to 55%. Access to affordable childcare has also made it increasingly difficult for working parents as childcare providers have decreased by 10% compared to pre-pandemic levels. Five states, including Alaska, Arkansas, Arizona, Missouri, and Texas, missed out on nearly 2.7 billion dollars because of the lack of childcare options within their economies. We can easily see the interconnections between our economy and isolated workforce challenges. Research may show that specific demographics are impacted, but the reality is that these challenges are all of ours to own. The workforce impacts and is impacted by businesses, schools, institutions, governments, and more.

FINDING AND DEVELOPING TALENT FOR ORGANIZATIONS (INTERNAL)

Recruiting and retaining talent should and will continue to be a priority for organizations. However, I believe there should be a different approach and a more comprehensive approach when it comes to finding and developing the people that participate in the workforce. When it comes to finding and developing talent in the workforce, I propose two perspectives for organizations, which include an internal and external strategy. Internally, organizations can do the following:

- Create, share, & champion vision
- Create internal work experience
- Create peer coaching opportunities
- Create learning communities
- Create career pathways
- Force leaders to emerge

Leaders must create a vision, share the vision, and constantly champion their vision. Leaders have a priority to make companies more profitable for their shareholders. There's no question that the priority for leaders is to sell and deliver the product or service to its customers. However, many leaders have underestimated the power of intrinsic motivation to help increase productivity and profitability. By creating, sharing, and championing the vision of the organization gives the people who work for the organization the opportunity to buy in and do the work needed. When organizations have a vision that allows people to buy in fully, this correlates to not only improving profitably but also the sustainability of a company's workforce. This may seem silly to say, but you wouldn't believe how many companies neglect their vision. Maintaining the status quo and the old way of doing things will bring inevitable drift to any organization. Vision provides goals, alignment, and organizational values, and it eventually provides best practices that professionals can adopt in order to execute the vision. Vision is important because it helps tackle retention-related workforce challenges. If you want to retain your most talented employees or diverse talent, then create a vision in which they can see themselves. No matter how technically talented a person is, they are wired to see how they contribute to a greater purpose. Vision is a bridge that allows people to participate in their purpose while working to develop the skills to continue contributing to their purpose. Leaders should create visions that align with the services the organization delivers and the people that deliver those services.

Organizations can create internal work experience opportunities to solve workforce challenges. Our education systems have helped inadvertently create a specialty mindset in the workforce. Students find their majors and work towards a niche job function or role in a company. We need highly technical skilled professionals. The gaps we have in our workforce are evidence of a lack of highly skilled individuals in organizations. I don't propose a solution that gets rid of education and training opportunities where these skills gaps aren't addressed. Rather, I propose one option of organizations creating internal work experience opportunities to address those skills gaps. Companies can provide cross-functional job experiences, shadowing, and enrichment in order to address workforce gaps. Having professionals work with a specialist in another area of the company can lead to individuals gaining skills and experience that solve the organization's talent issues. Obviously, this takes strategy and collaboration. For a growing company that doesn't have the infrastructure to execute the primary business model, this might not be a good option. For organizations at scale that have less of a problem with the economics of delivering their services and more of a challenge recruiting and retaining talent, giving internal work experience can be a solution.

Creating peer coaching opportunities is a great way for an organization's talent to grow and for a company to champion its culture. Mentorships will happen organically as people connect with folks they look up to or would like to learn from. Companies can harness this natural human tendency through formal peer coaching opportunities. Peer coaching can be structured between job functions, between teams within business units, cross-functional project collaborations, built into orientation processes, built into annual performance evaluations, and much more. Most organizations have a Human Resources department that either has a staff member who specializes in Training and Development or has a separate team that focuses on Training and Development. Leaders can partner with their Talent and Development department to assess, design, and implement peer coaching systems within the organization.

Like mentorship, learning communities happen informally and organically within organizations. People will always lean on each other for help, learning new skills, technology, and systems and getting clarity on how to perform better. Having intentional learning communities structured within the organization affirms that the company values the constant learning of its professionals. Learning communities can be centered around business units, departments, job functions, or more. Leaders can partner with Talent and Development departments to assess, design, and implement learning communities within the organization. Since many professionals leave organizations because they want opportunities for advancement, opportunities to lead, and opportunities to gain new skills, learning communities can be a great vehicle to retain those folks.

As a career coach, I don't believe it is the organization's job to help a professional manage their career. I strongly believe that the ownership lies with us individually, to constantly advocate and position ourselves for the advancement of our careers. Unfortunately, many professionals have grown codependent on organizations to fulfill their career goals. If we had the mindset that we are the owners of our careers, then I believe most of us can easily get unstuck in our careers. Though it is the individual's responsibility to manage their careers, companies can retain their workforce by creating clear career pathways within the organization. These pathways are going to be forever changing and difficult to define. Some of us are called to be specialists, managers, executives, and various job functions that organizations have. A career pathway from specialist to executive isn't a path that everyone would want to travel. Again, it is not the organization's responsibility to provide a pathway for all of its employees to follow.

Organizations owe it to themselves to do what is in their best interest to ethically sustain their mission. Organizations have a responsibility to their shareholders and/or stakeholders, but not at the expense of sustaining itself. Everything under the sun has a shelf life, including organizations. My point of emphasis is less about the ethical dilemmas companies must navigate around their business model and more on their relationship with their employees. Apart from the owner or founder of an organization, there isn't a person inside of the organization who is not subject to accountability for their performance. From top management to middle managers to frontline employees, every person in the organization must be accountable for the work they do. Organizations should force leaders to emerge. The hard truth is that many companies have passively appeased underperforming employees rather than nudging leaders to rise to the top. Finding and developing talent should not be at the expense of insulating people who are not champions of the company's vision and performing to execute that vision. If educators, leaders, and workforce development professionals are truth-tellers with humility, empathy, and a dedication to performing at a standard of excellence, then they will help leaders emerge. This will attract and retain the best talent, contributing to a sustainable workforce.

FINDING AND DEVELOPING TALENT FOR ORGANIZATIONS (EXTERNAL)

There isn't a one-size-fits-all approach to finding and developing talent within our organizations. Leaders will have to develop strategies internally and externally with respect to the companies they serve. Coaches play a significant role in both of those strategies, as no matter what job function people serve, they will utilize coaching in some shape or fashion to develop talent. When I first started Lenore Coaching LLC, I learned pretty quickly how desperate professionals are to find the right career and company that fits their goals. The reasons for people leaving their organizations ranged from wanting a higher salary, wanting more of a challenge, feeling disengaged and unappreciated, company culture, leadership styles, and much more. At Lenore Coaching, it was great being able to help professionals accelerate their careers or pivot to new careers altogether. Often, the folks I'd work with were so overwhelmed and anxious that their career transition increased their mental health and overall quality of life immediately. However, I realized that the impact I had was limited to just one person at a time. I found myself tackling the same challenge after another with each one of my clients. When I zoomed out, I saw the potential and need to better serve our workforce at scale. The strategies I share have the potential to impact the lives of so many people while simultaneously helping organizations. The secret sauce is in collaboration. The Purpose Driven Coaching model is meant to provide value individually but at scale to all of us collectively. External ways that organizations can find and develop talent include:

- Collaboration between education and businesses
- Experiential learning programs
- Educate future workforce participants

When I worked in Higher Education, I saw a synergistic relationship between Career Services offices and businesses that came on campus to recruit college students. On-campus recruiting programs have slight variations from campus to campus, but for the most part, they are the same. Career Service departments would host a number of career fairs on their campus. Staff members who work in Career Services departments typically include Employer Development professionals, Career Advisors, and Marketing & Outreach Specialists. Together, these folks would host career fairs where they funnel students from various academic programs who might be interested in internships, part-time jobs, and full-time jobs within career fields of interest. From the student perspective, this is often a time when they are learning about job functions, organizations, and industries. They are learning about the necessary skills and experience needed to potentially work at specific organizations. Most importantly, I believe this is an opportunity for these students to communicate professionally to gain information, build rapport, and articulate their stories to actual employers. From the employer perspective, Career Service departments try to attract employers that align with the career pathways that academic programs offer on campus. Employers that provide quality job opportunities and have reputations for good organizational cultures are usually the types of employers that Career Service departments look to attract. There are other collaborations that universities have with businesses, including information sessions, classroom events, roundtable events, career treks, and interviews. All these engagement opportunities between college students and employers are meant to provide value to both audiences, which ultimately contribute to the development of our workforce.

On-campus recruiting programming isn't a perfect system, but it is a great example of what collaboration can look like between educational institutions and businesses. These collaborations do not have to be exclusive to Higher Education, but there is much potential at all levels of education for partnerships with businesses. There are over 3 million students who graduate high school each year. Nearly 40% of all high school graduates, regardless of the current education and career they have chosen, are deeply unsure about what they want to do with their future. The Bureau of Labor Statistics reports that although workers under the age of 25 represent only one-fifth of hourly-paid workers, they make up almost 50% of workers who are paid the federal minimum wage or less. Simply put, a career working in low-wage jobs is the most likely prospect for high school graduates if our education systems and businesses do not strategically partner together.

Experiential learning is a great vehicle for businesses to partner with educational institutions by providing workforce-specific value to young people. Lenore Coaching LLC partners with the Mayor's Youth Academy in Richmond, Virginia, delivering career readiness programming to youth between the ages of 12 - 19 years old. The Mayor's Youth Academy coordinates a comprehensive employment program with local businesses where youth work over six weeks in the summer. The funding comes from the local government's budget to pay the students an hourly wage. The businesses provide work opportunities, mentorship, and coaching from the staff that supervise the students. Lenore Coaching provides career readiness programming to the students to provide coaching for professionalism, career clarity, and long-term goal setting. Lenore Coaching also provides training to the supervisors in those businesses to ensure that each employer is able to provide a professional experience for the students and the supervisors. The synergy in this relationship is apparent. Three different partners collaborate together to equip young people with the tools to have careers beyond low-wage employment opportunities. This program arguably helps to build a talent pipeline for the employer partners that participate. This model can be replicated across governments, schools, institutions, and businesses.

If our education systems and institutions aren't going anywhere, then it is time that we change it from within. As a teenager, the images of success were my parents. I was blessed to have examples of successful parents and to have conversations about having a career. They set an expectation for me that I needed to figure out a plan for my life. Sports was my initial ticket to get to college, but because of their lifelong coaching, I knew that I needed to figure out something beyond sports. Many young people don't have the level of privilege that I had, where education about career readiness is commonplace. There is a tremendous opportunity for businesses to find and develop talent by helping to educate the future workforce. This can be done in a plethora of ways, including but limited to through social media, providing training to schools and educators, and offering training for in-demand skills in the workforce. Google is a great example of a global company that has made great efforts in educating the current and future workforce. Google provides self-paced learning where individuals can get certifications in Cybersecurity, Data Analytics, Digital Marketing and e-commerce, Information Technology Support, Project Management, & UX Design. These certifications were meant for folks who have no foundational knowledge in these areas who want to establish careers within those industries. Google created a $100 million fund in partnership with three organizations to attempt to drive $1 billion in wage gains for low-wage workers. Their goal is to contribute to the development of the workforce by helping to educate people through training and collaboration with other organizations. I currently work for a company called Merit America, which is a recipient of a large portion of the Google fund. Merit America is a nonprofit company that provides career readiness programming to low-wage workers to help individuals gain the soft skills and job search strategy tools necessary to make a transition into in-demand tech jobs. In my role, I get to lead a team of coaches that provide coaching to individuals who are transitioning from low-wage jobs to a new tech career. The work that Google is doing can easily be modeled in other education systems and institutions. Businesses have a tremendous opportunity to find and develop talent for the workforce by being a part of the solution.

PARTNERING & COACHING WITHIN THE EDUCATION SYSTEM

The role of the coach has a lot of potential in today's education system. School districts have realized that selling students on a pathway to college isn't for everyone. Many students aren't academically ready for college, aren't interested in college, or don't want to deal with the astronomical cost associated with going to college. Students and educators know that different paths to the workforce are important now more than ever. Over the past decade, school districts have created their own technical centers that offer pathways for students to enter the workforce. Some of the programs offered within these technical centers include agriculture, automotive, construction, cosmetology, barbering, culinary arts, manufacturing, health science, information technology, law, public safety, and more. Offering these programs presents a tremendous opportunity for students and the development of the workforce. Despite these offerings, these programs are underutilized. Many students either don't know they have access to these programs or they can't leverage these opportunities because they don't have clarity on their own career goals. Teachers, School Counselors, and other staff members are either not equipped or don't have the bandwidth in their roles to provide necessary coaching to help students leverage workforce programs through technical centers. School districts have room for growth by hiring career coaches to guide students through appropriate workforce-related decision-making or by equipping Teachers, School Counselors, and staff members with skills and resources to provide coaching to their students.

Lenore Coaching partnered with a high school through a grant funded by a school district. For roughly six months, we provided coaching and facilitation to 102 sophomores within a specific English class. This partnership was brokered through my relationship with an English teacher who saw the need for her students to gain career readiness skills and explore opportunities in the workforce. Prior to the program, 67% of the students felt at least moderately prepared to go into a career, while 33% of the students felt unprepared to go into a career. Upon completion of the program, 82% of the students felt at least moderately prepared to go into a career, while only 18% of the students felt they were unprepared to go into a career. These data points show the impact of the work we did by providing career readiness in a large group setting. If this program collaborated with the technical center, it would be easy to create avenues for students to explore workforce-related pathways. Unfortunately, politics within our education systems often create barriers instead of knocking down barriers for our students. When we piloted this program with the English class, we built a business case that included all of our data and program methods to bring to key stakeholders of the technical center within the school district. This program was brought with immediate pushback because the leaders felt like our program infringed upon their efforts. The reality is that the technical center is a resource that very few students know about. The professionals who educate students on participating in the technical center don't focus on providing career readiness coaching or training to help students see how their interests could connect to the program offerings. Education systems are notorious for being territorial. Educators, leaders, and workforce development professionals will see the best impact when we work collaboratively to accomplish our mission. Territorialism and closed mindsets will only continue to proliferate the talent gaps in our workforce. The Purpose Driven Coaching model emphasizes a collective effort that allows us to address our individual gaps as coaches while leveraging the strength of partnerships to accomplish our respective missions.

Within our education systems, the professionals who serve students face a lot of challenges they face. Many schools are underfunded and under-resourced. There are challenges that make it difficult for educators to do their primary jobs. Many educators are constantly putting out fires rather than investing their primary time and energy into educating students. I call this out because it isn't any fault of their own. I used to have a very strong opinion about the nature of our education systems. Previously, I used to think that we should throw out the entire system, and then I had kids. Every student has individual needs and comes from homes where their minds and behaviors are shaped. They bring all of their attitudes, beliefs, personalities, perspectives, and traumas to the school in which we expect our educators to work their magic. We expect educators to teach while managing a classroom with a handful of students who are disruptive. We expect administrators to hold teachers accountable when a small group of students defiantly disrespect educators in their classes. When administrators and teachers bring students' behavior to the attention of their parents or guardians, they make excuses for their child's behavior and misdirect the blame back on the educators. No one is perfect in this equation when it comes to educating and parenting our youth. However, I want to stress the importance that our educators and education systems are facing a huge challenge when it comes to educating and developing today's youth. My opinion about education has drastically changed over the past ten years. I look back at some of my past teachers and administrators, and I'm so glad that God put them in my life. I'm glad they held me accountable for those times when I was disengaged or when I had terrible classroom behavior. I'm glad that I had Ms. Archibald and Ms. Duncan to nudge me and love me at the same time. We can't throw the baby out with the bathwater. We have to transform it from within.

We expect School counselors to help each student transition from school to college or from school to the workforce, but they are not equipped to do so. School counselors have to schedule classes, administer standardized tests, provide social and emotional support, address concerns that interfere with learning, and provide school and community-based resources, all while helping each student to plan for postsecondary education and career options. Usually, there are 1 - 2 School counselors at a school that serve hundreds of students. School counselors are not career coaches. Even if those School counselors have career coaching knowledge and skills, they don't have the bandwidth to provide an individualized pathway for each student at the school. Collaboration isn't just a good idea, it's a necessary strategy when it comes to partnering and coaching within the education system.

HOW TO USE THIS BOOK

There are two ways that I'd like for you to use this book. All of us contribute to the workforce in various job functions. However, not many of us know what our calling is. Your calling is doing work that aligns with your purpose. All of our purposes are wrapped around loving God and honoring Him. Genesis 1:28 says, ***"God blessed them and said to them, "Be fruitful and increase in number; fill the earth and subdue it. Rule over the fish in the sea and the birds in the sky and over every living creature that moves on the ground."*** Through this scripture, we have 4 Pillars of Purpose, including the following:

- **Individual fruitfulness** - The work I do is productive, helpful, and impactful for me
- **Population fruitfulness** - The work I do is productive, helpful, and impactful for others
- **Territorial expansion** - The work I do leads to the growth of organizations, institutions, and geographies.

- **Territorial control** - The work I do has consistent productivity and impact on organizations, institutions, and geographies.

After reading this book, the first thing I would like for you to do is have an honest conversation with yourself and ask yourself if you're living out your calling. Your calling isn't married to a job title, organization, or industry. You should ask yourself, "Am I doing work that aligns with the Purpose Driven Coaching model?" If not, don't make a drastic lifestyle change immediately. But begin to assess your values, interests, and skills. Begin to tap into your network and research. Start to reflect and strategize how you can better live out your calling. Secondly, I hope that you assess your current role and brainstorm how you can use coaching in your role or enhance how you utilize coaching. Think about the content discussed in this book to see how you can leverage the coaching principles within it. Some ideas you can begin to adopt include but are not limited to:

- Applying the PDC model
- Understanding how to use coaching vs. counseling, consulting, and mentoring
- Using Strengths-based coaching
- Leveraging the Prototype Process
- Understanding your unique discontent
- Asking the right questions

I can't thank you enough for walking on this journey with me. All of us have an important role to play in our world of work. There isn't a job too prestigious or too trivial where our impact is not felt. Every human interaction and experience we have with one another shapes us. Coaching is a strategic instrument where we shape people from a position of purpose and shape people with purpose. I am very mindful of how tricky it can be to navigate faith or religious identities when it comes to our world of work. On my journey, I have realized how much God desires for us to be a part of our lives and how much he desires for us to enjoy the places we play and work. There isn't any intellect or territory that is beyond the grasp of God of his power and glory. The Purpose Driven Coaching model is a tool inspired by God's Spirit and the scripture. Without even knowing it, most of us have transformed lives, organizations, and industries using the PDC model. I pray for much success in your life and in the work you do. Subdue and multiply!

SOURCES

Chapter 1
1. https://www.foxsports.com/stories/nba/lebron-james-record-tracker-how-far-is-he-from-kareem-abdul-jabbar#:~:text=LeBron%20James%20passes%20Kareem%20Abdul%2DJabbar%20for%20NBA%20career%20scoring%20record,-Updated%20Feb.&text=Los%20Angeles%20Lakers%20superstar%20LeBron,Tuesday%2C%20February%207%2C%202023.
2. https://olympics.com/en/news/dirk-nowitzki-dallas-mavericks-career-stats-records-numbers
3. https://www.nba.com/news/pat-rileys-nineteen-nba-finals-timeline
4. https://www.nbclosangeles.com/news/sports/everything-to-know-about-miami-heat-coach-erik-spoelstra/3161894/#:~:text=How%20many%20championships%20has%20Erik,appearances%20from%2020 11%20to%202014.
5. https://www.pujolasos.com/en/teamexcellence/#:~:text=%E2%80%9CTalent%20wins%20games%2C%20but%20teamwork,(Michael%20Jordan)
6. https://bestsellingalbums.org/album/371
7. https://www.forbes.com/sites/hughmcintyre/2023/07/12/btss-jimin-and-suga-and-taylor-swift-the-10-bestselling-albums-at-2023s-midway-point/
8. https://www.the-numbers.com/movie/Get-Rich-or-Die-Tryin#tab=summary
9. Curtis Jackon, *Hustle Harder Hustle Smarter* (New York, New York: HarperCollins Publishers, 2020)
10. https://www.danbeverly.com/brain-based-coaching/
11. Genesis 1:28 (NLT)

Chapter 2
1. Stacy Spikes, *Black Founder: The hidden power of being an outsider* (New York, New York: Kensington Publishing Corp. 2023)
2. Lecrae Moore, *Church Clothes 4 Tour.* (Liberation Church, Richmond, Virginia 2023
3. https://www.youtube.com/@progressive
4. Tony Evans, *Kingdom Men Rising.* (Bloomington, Minnesota: BethanyHouse, 2021)

Chapter 3
1. Babin, L; Willink, J. *Extreme Ownership: How U.S. Navy Seals Lead and Win* (New York, New York: St. Martin's Press, 2017)
2. https://www.merriam-webster.com/dictionary/skill#:~:text=%3A%20the%20ability%20to%20use%20one's,a%20developed%20aptitude%20or%20ability
3. https://www.talentguard.com/blog/whats-difference-skills-competencies
4. https://www.investopedia.com/terms/s/soft-skills.asp
5. https://www.statista.com/statistics/273575/us-average-cost-incurred-by-a-data-breach/#:~:text=As%20of%202023%2C%20the%20average,million%20U.S.%20dollars%20in%202023.
6. https://www.indeed.com/hire/c/info/cost-of-hiring-employees#:~:text=However%2C%20most%20companies%20can%20expect,the%20position%20and%20your%20company.
7. https://uk.indeed.com/career-advice/career-development/how-to-teach-skills
8. https://www.aplu.org/our-work/4-policy-and-advocacy/publicuvalues/employment-earnings/#:~:text=The%20earnings%20gap%20between%20college,earnings%20are%20%2430%2C000%20a%20year.
9. https://www.gallup.com/cliftonstrengths/en/253754/history-cliftonstrengths.aspx
10. Evans, J; Kelsey, A, *Strengths Based Marriage: Building a stronger relationship by understanding each other's gifts* (Nashville, Tennessee: Nelson Books, 2016)

Chapter 4

1. https://www.google.com/url?q=https://www.cnbc.com/video/2021/02/06/how-tesla-was-founded-martin-eberhard-and-marc-tarpenning-tell-all.html&sa=D&source=docs&ust=1695738191955822&usg=AOvVaw2z7N1LXfUfUAJC1eUMZlhp

2. Barack Obama, *A Promised Land* (New York, New York:Random House, 2020)

3. https://languages.oup.com/google-dictionary-en/

4. https://www.cars.com/research/tesla/#:~:text=Current%20vehicles%20include%20the%20Model,more%20than%20%24100%2C000%20when%20new.

5. Jon Acuff, *Quitter: Closing the gap between your day job & your dream job* (Brentwood, Tennessee: Lampo Press 2011)

Chapter 5

1. Vad Lee, *Purpose over Position* (Franklin, Tennessee: Carpenter's Son Publishing, 2020)

2. https://jmusports.com/sports/football/roster/vad-lee/8778

3. https://www.sports-reference.com/cfb/players/vad-lee-1.html

4. https://ramblinwreck.com/georgia-tech-football-vad-lee/

5. Dharius Daniels, *Your Purpose is Calling* (Grand Rapids, Michigan: Zondervan, 2022)

6. Garcia, H; Miralles, F, *Ikigai: The Japanese Secret to a Long and Happy Life* (New York, New York: Penguin Books, 2016)

7. https://nccc.georgetown.edu/curricula/awareness/index.html

8. https://nccc.georgetown.edu/bias/module-3/1.php#:~:text=This%20type%20of%20bias%20is,subtle%20means%20such%20as%20exclusion.

Chapter 6
1. https://www.npr.org/2023/09/15/1199321274/lehman-brothers-collapse-2008-mortgages
2. https://www.cnbc.com/2023/07/31/ai-could-affect-many-white-collar-high-paid-jobs.html
3. https://www.forbes.com/sites/markcperna/2022/02/15/americas-education-crisis-is-costing-us-our-school-leadership-what-are-we-going-to-do-about-it/?sh=6e2d37031f25
4. https://housingmatters.urban.org/research-summary/addressing-americas-affordable-housing-crisis
5. https://www.cbsnews.com/news/why-college-is-so-expensive-and-what-can-be-done-about-it/
6. https://hbr.org/2022/03/is-remote-work-actually-better-for-the-environment
7. https://genius.com/Tina-turner-whats-love-got-to-do-with-it-lyrics
8. https://www.smartdraw.com/pyramid-charts/examples/traditional-organization-pyramid-chart/
9. https://www.glassdoor.com/Career/executive-career_KO0,9.htm#:~:text=Executives%20are%20the%20top%20employees,and%20working%20on%20company%20policies.
10. Society for Human Resource Management, *2019 SHRM Learning System* (Alexandria, VA 2019). shrm.org

Chapter 7
1. James 2:17 (NLT)
2. https://www.linkedin.com/pulse/top-100-hiring-statistics-2022-rinku-thakkar/
3. https://www.businesswire.com/news/home/20230124005054/en/Skills-Gap-Rapidly-Widening-According-to-New-Wiley-Survey#:~:text=Among%20600%20U.S.%20human%20resources,executive%20vice%20president%20at%20Wiley.
4. https://www.cnbc.com/2023/05/26/employers-are-learning-gen-z-isnt-the-easiest-generation-to-work-with.html

5. https://www.uschamber.com/workforce/understanding-americas-labor-shortage

6. https://www.uschamberfoundation.org/sites/default/files/Equity_ChildCare_Final_web.pdf

7. https://www.pewresearch.org/short-reads/2021/11/04/amid-the-pandemic-a-rising-share-of-older-u-s-adults-are-now-retired/

8. https://www.uschamber.com/workforce/the-states-suffering-most-from-the-labor-shortage

9. https://www.avature.net/blogs/6-tips-to-combat-the-post-pandemic-talent-shortage/

10. https://hbr.org/2020/01/how-the-best-managers-identify-and-develop-talent

11. https://www.cnbc.com/2023/01/18/70percent-of-gen-z-and-millennials-are-considering-leaving-their-jobs-soon.html

12. https://districtadministration.com/college-and-career-decisions-high-school-graduates-not-ready-youscience/#:~:text=37%25%20of%20the%20graduates%E2%80%94regardless,planned%20educational%20or%20career%20path.

13. https://www.thinkimpact.com/high-school-statistics/#:~:text=High%20School%20Graduation%20Rates&text=It%20is%20estimated%20that%203%2C650%2C000,of%20states'%20graduation%20rates%20increased.

14. https://www.bls.gov/opub/reports/minimum-wage/2020/home.htm#:~:text=Among%20hourly%20paid%20workers%20age,a%20bachelor's%20degree%20and%20higher.

15. https://grow.google/

16. https://blog.google/outreach-initiatives/grow-with-google/career-certificates-fund/

17. https://meritamerica.org/about/google-career-certificates-fund/

ABOUT THE AUTHOR

Quintrel Lenore also known as "Q" is an author and coach focused on career readiness, workforce development, and organizational leadership. He has worked with hundreds of educators, leaders, and workforce development professionals who have used his coaching methods and programs. Through his company Lenore Coaching LLC, Quintrel has a program called "Momentum" which is a career readiness and workforce development program that has served over 500 youth. This program has partnered with local government agencies, nonprofit organizations, and school districts to help youth by creating pathways into the workforce.

Q champions the Purpose Driven Coaching model as a tool to help professionals align purpose within their world of work. His work with the PDC model has appeared in front of thousands of professionals through organizations such as the National Association of Workforce Development Professionals, the National Urban League, Society for Human Resource Professionals, the Virginia Association of Colleges and Employers, and more.

Lenore is an avid Hip Hop enthusiast who enjoys listening to music and creating music of his own.

LENORE COACHING
PURPOSE DRIVEN LIVING

We are coaches and training & development professionals with over 10 years of experience helping individuals align and maximize their calling with their purpose. We also help organizations create innovative solutions to educate and build a sustainable workforce.

**Momentum
Career & Workforce
Readiness**

**Leadership &
Professional
Development**

**Speaking,
Facilitation, &
Coaching**

**Curriculum &
Courses**

Visit and connect with us at www.lenorecoaching.com

Made in the USA
Middletown, DE
02 October 2023